S O S

STORIES OF SURVIVAL

SOS

STORIES OF SURVIVAL

True Tales of Disaster, Tragedy, and Courage

By Ed Butts

Tundra Books

Published in Canada by Tundra Books,
75 Sherbourne Street, Toronto, Ontario M5A 2P9

Published in the United States by Tundra Books of Northern New York,
P. O. Box 1030, Plattsburgh, New York 12901

Library of Congress Control Number: 2006904823

National Library of Canada Cataloguing in Publication

Butts, Edward, 1951–
SOS : stories of survival / Ed Butts.

ISBN 978-0-88776-786-9

1. Child disaster victim—Juvenile literature.   2. Disaster
victims—Juvenile literature.   I. Title.

D24.B88 2007   J363.34   C2006-902984-9

ONTARIO ARTS COUNCIL
CONSEIL DES ARTS DE L'ONTARIO

We acknowledge the financial support of the Government of Canada through the Book
Publishing Industry Development Program (BPIDP) and that of the Government of Ontario
through the Ontario Media Development Corporation's Ontario Book Initiative.
We further acknowledge the support of the Canada Council for the Arts and the
Ontario Arts Council for our publishing program.

Text design: Beate Schwirtlich
Printed and bound in Canada

This book is printed on acid-free paper that is 100% recycled,
ancient-forest friendly (100% post-consumer recycled)

2 3 4 5 6   12 11 10 09 08

For Austin, my grandson

CONTENTS

INTRODUCTION

Everybody's life is touched at some time by disaster. It could be something as temporary as the loss of a big game or an initial failure to achieve a desired goal. Or it can be something as deeply felt and permanent as the death of a loved one. There are some disasters, however, that are felt universally. These are the disasters that leave us shocked and sometimes angry and that move us to do something to help, even if we do not live in the places where they have occurred, nor personally know any of the people involved. Almost everyone who heard of the events had an emotional reaction to the destruction wrought by Hurricane Katrina, the devastation caused by a tsunami in Southeast Asia, and the brutal terrorist acts of September 11, 2001. In each instance, millions of people responded to the call for aid.

Some disasters are natural: an earthquake or a hurricane strikes a populated area. Some disasters are man-made: a dropped match starts a deadly fire in a building full of people. War, too, is a man-made disaster. Many disasters are a combination of both. A flood caused by a violent storm is certainly natural. But if death and property damage result because a poorly constructed dam breaks, then there is also a human contribution.

Nobody can prevent natural phenomena such as hurricanes, earthquakes, and volcanic eruptions. But unlike our ancestors, we have the technology to predict them with at least some degree of accuracy, and can be prepared for them. Buildings in earthquake-prone regions are constructed to resist tremors. People are evacuated from the path of a hurricane.

Man-made disasters are almost always preventable. They are usually the result of shortsightedness, stupidity, or greed. A movie-house owner overcrowds his establishment and ignores fire safety regulations. A man-made reservoir is filled beyond the limits of safety so that a privileged few can enjoy sailing. A mining company sends underpaid boys underground in order to maximize profits.

All of the disaster stories presented in this volume focus upon the young people who were involved. Some of them were heroes. Others had miraculous escapes. All, in one way or another, were victims; sometimes of the elements; sometimes of human exploitation. While all of these stories tell of historical disasters, we, the first people of the twenty-first century, must bear in mind that the conditions that spawned them are still with us. Children in Third World countries still work under conditions like those of the Triangle Shirtwaist Factory, and the products of their toil are sold in our stores. Many nations do not have the economies to construct defenses against natural calamities. Scientists have warned that the effects of global warming are already wreaking havoc with planet Earth. There are still measures that must be taken so that tragedies such as those described in these chapters might be reduced in impact, or even prevented

I

· · · — — · · ·

THE ASIA
"THE BOAT IS DOOMED!"

Today, many people regard the waters and shores of North America's Great Lakes as summer vacation playgrounds, but in the nineteenth century the five linked lakes were the continent's principal transportation route. Roads were rough and traveling them was painfully slow. Railroads were still in their infancy, especially on the rugged north shores of the lakes. The most convenient way to move people and goods was by water. Every year millions of tons of farm produce, timber, ore, and manufactured goods — as well as thousands of passengers — crossed these inland seas in sailing vessels and steamboats.

Saltwater sailors tended to look down their noses at the freshwater sailors of the Great Lakes. Compared to the vast oceans they sailed, these old salts considered the lakes mere puddles. They changed their tune when they had to navigate the "puddles" of Lake Ontario, Erie, Huron, Michigan, or Superior, though. These confined bodies of water were often a mariner's nightmare. Tricky crosswinds could turn a routine voyage into a life and death struggle. Storms blew up with a suddenness that astonished even the most experienced of sailors. There wasn't much room to maneuver a ship in bad weather and the lakes were mostly uncharted. A gauntlet of reefs and shoals lurked beneath the waves, ready to tear the bottoms out of ships. Still, if you wanted to go from Duluth, Minnesota, say, to Kingston, Ontario, there was really only one way. And maybe the weather would be fair all the way. Maybe!

~~~

Seventeen-year-old Christy Ann Morrison was feeling seasick the morning of Thursday, September 14, 1882, as the passenger steamer *Asia* pitched and rolled in the rough waters of Georgian Bay, the huge extension of Lake Huron that is almost as big as Lake Ontario. Christy was too ill to eat breakfast. She recalled the old saying about seasickness: "First you feel like you're going to die, then you wish you would." She must also have heard that it was better to stay out in the open air than below in a bunk, because Christy remained on deck. Her cabin mates were also seasick, but had stayed in their bunks. They were suffering miserably as the ship rose and fell on the angry waters. Christy could not have known as she fought down nausea that she was about to endure an ordeal much worse than seasickness.

The *Asia* was a large steamer, approximately 136 feet (41.5 m) long and 23 feet (7 m) in the beam (the widest part of the deck). Though she had been in service for nine years, the *Asia* had not been built for the open water of the Great Lakes, but was actually of riverboat design. Officially she was allowed to carry no more than forty passengers, in addition to a crew of twenty-four. On that fateful September day there were more than 100 passengers crowded aboard the ship.

The *Asia's* skipper, John N. Savage, had been sailing the Great Lakes for twelve years, but he'd been a captain for only one year. Two months earlier, the ship's owners had sent Captain Savage a letter giving him strict orders to keep his vessel in shelter whenever the weather was bad. Perhaps Captain Savage did not fully understand these instructions. Some people claimed that he was illiterate.

On September 13 the *Asia* had already encountered rough weather. One passenger later reported hearing ". . . cracking sounds . . . as if she were being torn assunder . . . and then a loud report . . . as if the vessel had burst in two." When they put in to the harbor at the town of Owen Sound, a steamboat inspector examined the *Asia* and told Captain Savage, ". . . . she'll never get to French River, as she is strained." The captain argued with the inspector and dismissed the warning. Moments later, Christy Ann Morrison boarded the *Asia,* bound for Sault Ste. Marie. She had every expectation of a safe journey. After all, her cousin John McDonald was First Mate.

Also on board the *Asia* as it sailed from Owen Sound at about midnight was Douglas Albert Tinkis, 18, who was traveling with his uncle, J.H. Tinkis. In all likelihood the boy and his uncle were returning to their home on Manitoulin Island after a visit to Owen Sound.

The sky was overcast as the *Asia* sailed down the sound toward the open water of Georgian Bay, but the waters were relatively calm. The ship made a brief stop at Presqu'ile Point to take on wood for the boiler and hay for ten horses that were on the main deck at the bow. Most of the passengers, whose number included nine children, slept soundly through what would be their last night on earth.

At about 8:00 on the morning of the 14th, a storm swept across the bay and suddenly the steamer was being tossed by heavy seas. Sailors knew from past experience that in rough weather the *Asia* did not "answer the helm well" (meaning that the ship was difficult to steer). Now the crew found their ship at the mercy of a storm that was building up to gale force. Douglas Tinkis, still unaware that there was any real danger, ate his breakfast. Most of the other passengers were too seasick to think of food.

For almost three hours the *Asia*'s crew battled the raging seas. Christy Ann asked her cousin, the First Mate, if they were going to sink. McDonald said that they had already pushed the horses overboard and if necessary they would jettison the cargo to lighten the ship. Christy Ann saw some people putting on life preservers, but many of the passengers were so incapacitated by seasickness they seemed simply to not care what happened to them. By this time, just before 11:00, Christy Ann was so ill she felt she had to lie down. She went back to her stateroom and crawled onto her bunk.

At about the same time Douglas Tinkis, who had returned to his stateroom, heard his uncle's cry of alarm. "Duga! The boat is doomed!" Huge waves were crashing over the *Asia,* tearing the already strained timbers apart. The inspector's unheeded warning to Captain Savage was turning into a horrible reality. The *Asia* hadn't a chance of making it to French River.

J.H. Tinkis would not survive the shipwreck, but his warning to "Duga" may well have saved his nephew's life. Douglas rushed out of his stateroom, pulling on his hat and coat as he ran. When he realized that the ship was foundering, Douglas dashed back and put on a life preserver. Suddenly the ship listed dangerously to the starboard (right) side and the upper works broke away from the hull. Douglas hurried back out on deck and jumped over the port (left) side. He managed to pull himself into a lifeboat in which there were about twenty other people.

When Christy Ann Morrison saw water rushing into her stateroom, she realized that the ship was actually sinking. Seasick or not, she had to get out! First she ran into the adjoining stateroom and tried to rouse a woman who was either asleep or prostrate with seasickness. She later said that she did not think the woman even left the stateroom.

Christy Ann pulled on a life preserver and stumbled out on deck. The *Asia* had already rolled over on the starboard side. The girl slid down a rail into the water and sank. When she came up again, she was right beside a lifeboat. In it were Captain Savage, First Mate McDonald, the two women from her stateroom and some other men. The captain grabbed Christy Ann by the arm and pulled her into the boat. Her cousin told her to hold tightly to the boat's lifeline and not let go, no matter what.

As the *Asia* disappeared beneath the waves, scores of people struggled in the water or tried to swim to one of three lifeboats the crew had been able to launch. Christy Ann's boat had a pair of oars, but one of the the others had only a single oar and the third had none at all. The people in those two boats were helpless before the onslaught of the monstrous waves. Both boats flipped over. The boats would right themselves after capsizing, but each time it happened, people were lost.

Douglas Tinkis was thrown into the water again. His life preserver kept him afloat, but desperate people were grabbing at it and pulling the boy down. He pulled the life preserver off, and climbed back into the boat. There were so many people clinging to it that Douglas dove back into the water and swam to another boat. No sooner had he climbed in than it, too, flipped over.

Thus far Christy Ann's boat had remained upright. She saw the other two boats each capsize several times. People kept climbing back into them, but in fewer and fewer numbers. Finally, both boats were empty.

Then Christy Ann's boat overturned. She clung to the lifeline, just as McDonald had told her, and so stayed with the boat. Only seven people dragged themselves back into the craft: Christy Ann, Captain Savage, First Mate McDonald, a man named McAlpine, a man named John Little, an unidentified man – and Douglas Tinkis! Determined to survive, the teenager had swum to the lifeboat through furious seas after everyone else in his boat had perished.

Now only seven of the *Asia's* people were left, and their situation was not good. The lifeboat was upright, but the water was knee-deep, and there was no bailing bucket. All were wet and chilled to the bone, and a cold wind was blowing. First Mate McDonald fished an oar out of the water, but no one had the strength to use it.

The lifeboat drifted south as the storm died down. After sunset the people in it could see the lights of a town in the distance; probably Byng Inlet. But the castaways were at the mercy of the current, and the town might as well have been a hundred miles away.

In the darkness the men began to die, probably from exposure and exhaustion. "They seemed to go to sleep," Christy Ann said later. The unidentified man went first, followed by Mr. McAlpine and John Little. Then death came for Christy Ann's cousin.

"The mate put his head up to my face in the dark, and asked if it was me. I said 'Yes.' My hair was flying around and he seized it in his death grip and pulled down my head. I asked the captain, who was near, to release my hair. He did so, and the mate soon breathed his last. Shortly after the mate died the captain laid his head down. I tried to arouse him, but he was dead. I think this was about midnight."

Douglas and Christy Ann were now alone on the water in a boat full of dead men. She sat in the bow and he in the stern. Christy Ann was afraid that Douglas would go to sleep and die just like the men. She asked him to come to the bow and sit with her, but Douglas said it would balance the boat better if they stayed where they were. He promised he would not go to sleep.

All night the two young survivors kept up a conversation as the boat drifted with its grim cargo. Dawn revealed that they were near land, and the morning sun warmed them and dried their clothes. Using their single oar, Douglas maneuvered the boat to a rocky shore where he and Christy Ann at last set foot on solid ground.

They planned to travel on foot until they reached a community, but Christy Ann found that she could not walk. Douglas lifted the bodies out of the lifeboat and laid them on the shore. Then he dumped as much of the water as he could out of the boat. Christy Ann was too weakened to help him.

The two continued along the shore in the boat, but with only one oar they made very little progress. As night came on again, Christy Ann worried that the water would get rough. Douglas landed the boat on an island. There they made beds out of boughs and spent a chilly, hungry night.

Douglas and Christy Ann were up before sunrise. Once again they tried to row with the single oar, but by now neither of them had much strength left. They did not get very far. They stopped at another island where Christy Ann was sure they would die. Far off they could see what they thought was a lighthouse. Douglas said that maybe someone going to or from the tower would pass by and see them. The exhausted teenagers fell asleep on the rocks.

Half an hour later Douglas awoke with a start to see a Native person, whose name is not known, standing over him. He jumped up and asked the man if he had a boat. The man said that he had a sailboat. His wife was waiting with it at the other end of the island.

In return for Douglas' watch – which was probably waterlogged – the Natives agreed to take the youngsters to Parry Sound, about 22 miles (35.4 km) away. They gave Douglas some bread and pork, which he devoured. Christy Ann could not get any food down. She managed only to drink some cold tea. The woman made a bed for her in the bottom of the sailboat. On Sunday morning, three days after the shipwreck, the sole survivors of the *Asia* reached Parry Sound. There, according to Douglas, ". . . we were hospitably treated by the inhabitants."

When he had recovered from his ordeal, Douglas joined in the search for bodies from the *Asia,* hoping to find that of his uncle. A few bodies were recovered, but not the remains of J.H. Tinkis. Douglas' uncle was among the many claimed forever by Georgian Bay.

News of the wreck and the two teenagers' survival caused a great sensation. Holding a lifeline in her hands, Christy Ann posed for a dramatic photograph that became famous. People were amazed that a girl of 17 could survive a harrowing experience that had killed tough, veteran sailors. As time passed, however, Christy Ann became reluctant to talk about the shipwreck and the terrible days and nights that followed. Her moment of fame was too tragic to relive publicly time and time again.

This staged 1882 photo of Christy Ann Morrison, one of two survivors of the wreck of the *Asia,* became famous, but Christy Ann came to regret posing for it. She hated having to relive her ordeal in public time and time again.

Every one of the Great Lakes has at least one area called a "graveyard." No one knows exactly how many vessels lie on the cold, dark lakebeds, but the number runs into the thousands. With them lie the bones of the unfortunate people who went down with their ships. The wreck of the Asia *was one of the worst disasters that had ever happened on Georgian Bay. It brought about the enforcement of strict regulations regarding safety measures on Great Lakes ships, and the competency of ships' officers. Even though the evidence given by Christy Ann and Douglas indicated that the* Asia *had foundered in the storm, some government officials wondered if the ship might have struck one of the many uncharted shoals in Georgian*

Bay. As a direct result of the tragedy, the Canadian government embarked on an eleven-year project to completely survey and chart Georgian Bay. Future generations of mariners and passengers would be less likely to share the fate of the people on the doomed Asia.

2

. . . — — . . .

THE JOHNSTOWN FLOOD
"DON'T GO BACK FOR ANYTHING!"

In late May of 1889, a severe storm tore into western Pennsylvania. Quiet rivers became raging torrents and the water levels of lakes rose dramatically. High in the Allegheny Mountains, Lake Conemaugh, a man-made reservoir, swelled to over 20 million tons of water. In the valley below lay the community of Johnstown. All that stood between Johnstown's people and a major disaster was the South Fork Dam, about 14 miles (22.5 km up the Little Conemaugh River). This aging structure had been neglected for many years and a few voices had warned that the dam was in need of repair. But not many people really believed the dam would collapse. In fact, there was a standing joke in Johnstown and other valley communities: "Well, this is the day the old dam is going to break." On May 31, this was no joke.

~~~

Shortly before 4:00 PM on Friday, May 31, 1889, Horace Rose stood at a window on the second floor of his house and playfully used a broom to pass a piece of candy to Bessie Fronheiser. Eight-year-old Bessie was at the window of the house next door. After using the same trick to pass a cup of coffee to Bessie's mother, Horace Rose asked the little girl to come over and visit. She knew he was only teasing. It was pouring rain, the river was flooding, and the ground floors of both their houses were rapidly filling with water.

Horace had already complained to his wife that the water would ruin the new wallpaper downstairs, but he didn't think there was any real danger.

Johnstown had experienced floods before, and the water had never risen more than a few feet. Nonetheless, he had sent his son Forest to take the family's team of horses to higher ground. The younger Rose children, Percy, Winter, and June, were in the house with their parents.

Not far away 6-year-old Gertrude Quinn sat on the porch of her new brick home dangling her feet in the water. Her father, James, had given strict orders that everyone stay inside while he and his eldest son Vincent, 16, went to the family owned dry-goods store to move merchandise upstairs. But Gertrude wanted to watch the ducks that were swimming around in the front yard. In the house were Gertrude's older sisters, Helen and Rosemary, her little sister Marie who was sick with measles, her Aunt Abbie Geis, who was visiting with her baby son, Richard, and Libby Hipp, an 18-year-old nursemaid. Gertrude's mother and baby brother were out of town.

Unlike Horace Rose, James Quinn *was* very concerned about the flooding, and not just because of damage to his store. He was worried about the dam upriver. When he'd expressed his worries earlier in the day to Abbie, his sister-in-law had said, "James, you are too anxious. This big house could never go." James had considered taking everyone to higher ground, but was afraid of exposing little Marie to the foul weather.

Gertrude's father returned home just before 4:00 and scolded her for disobeying his instructions to stay inside. While the nursemaid took Gertrude to change into dry clothes and shoes, James told his family that they were going to the nearest hill. Then he went to the front door to flick ashes off his cigar.

Shortly before 4:00 George Heiser, owner of a general store, above which the family lived, sent his son Victor out to the barn to look after the horses. The animals were tied in their stalls, and on that stormy afternoon, with the waters rising, George thought that it would be better if they were free of their tethers. Sixteen-year-old Victor waded across the yard barefoot and went into the barn. It took him just a few minutes to do the job. He was about to dash back to the store when a noise such as he had never heard before stopped him at the barn door.

A few minutes before 4:00, Bill Heppenstall, 17, of Pittsburgh was a passenger on a train that was rolling into the village of Sang Hollow, 4 miles (6.4 km) downriver from Johnstown. When the train stopped, Bill and the other passengers learned that there was a problem with the line up ahead. For several minutes the railroad men talked over what they should do. Then, looking down on the swollen river that ran parallel with the tracks, they saw a startling sight rushing toward them from the direction of Johnstown.

With a population of about 15,000, Johnstown was a booming steel town in 1889. Set in the Conemaugh Valley, it was built on the flood plain of a river junction. Here the Little Conemaugh River met the Stony Creek River, and became the Conemaugh River. For most of the year these streams were tame, but in the spring they became raging torrents. The river channels that passed through Johnstown had actually been narrowed to make more building room. That meant that they were not wide enough to contain the volume of water produced by spring rains and thaw.

About 14 miles (22.5 km) up the Little Conemaugh was the South Fork Dam. Constructed of earth and rock, it had been built to hold a reservoir for a now abandoned canal. The dam was 72 feet (22 m) high, 220 feet (67 m) thick at the base, 20 feet (6 m) thick at the top, and stretched 918 feet (280 m) across the valley. At its eastern end there was an 85-foot (26-m) spillway through which water cascaded down into the valley. There had once been iron tubes at the base of the dam for water-level control, but by 1889 these had been removed.

Lake Conemaugh, behind the dam, was a little more than two miles (3.2 km) long and a mile (1.6 km) across at its widest point. Originally it was supposed to have been kept at a depth of 40 feet (12 m). After railroads put the canal out of business, the dam lay neglected for many years. In 1862 part of it washed away in a flood, but little damage was done in the valley below.

Then in 1879 a man named Benjamin Ruff bought the land around the lake – including the dam – and converted it into a resort called the South Fork Hunting and Fishing Club. He rebuilt the broken part of the dam, and allowed the lake level to rise to 70 feet (21.3 m). Ruff built a clubhouse and cottages, and stocked the lake with game fish. He put iron grates across the spillway to prevent the fish from escaping downstream. Wealthy businessmen such as Andrew Carnegie came to Lake Conemaugh to hunt, fish, and sail. The resort was off limits to local people. Groundskeepers chased off "poachers." This was at least in part the cause of strained relations between the rich people up on the mountain and the common folks down in the valley. So when people expressed concerns about the dam, Ruff chose to ignore them.

There was good cause for worry, though. The artificial lake was too big. People complained that the workmanship of the reconstructed part of the dam was substandard, and that the dam had started to sag in the middle. They warned that it would not hold if the volume of water increased. Ruff said that the dam was sound, and that the spillway was sufficient to handle any excess water.

Then came that slashing storm of May 30, 1889. It dumped record-breaking volumes of rain on the Alleghenies. Water coursed down mountainsides that had been denuded of trees by over-logging. It turned the little creeks that fed Lake Conemaugh into violent torrents that ripped away low-hanging tree branches. Lake Conemaugh began to rise. Its surface was littered with branches that the current carried toward the spillway. There they were snagged on the iron grates.

The downpour continued for the next two days. By the morning of Friday the 31st, the rivers were rising at the rate of a foot (.3 m) an hour. In Johnstown, first basements, and then ground floors were flooded. Men were sent home from work and children dismissed from school. Some anxious people headed for high ground. Many more simply went upstairs.

Back at the dam the situation had become critical. The spillway was hopelessly clogged with logs, branches, and other debris. Workmen furiously shoveled earth to try to heighten the dam. Another crew tried to hack out a new spillway. A young engineer named John Parke could see that both efforts would be futile. By 11:00 AM the water was slopping over the top of the dam.

Parke jumped on his horse and galloped down the muddy road to the nearest town, South Fork. When he told people that the dam was about to break, no one took him seriously. He sent a man to the railroad telegraph office with instructions to warn Johnstown. But the telegraph line between the communities was down.

At 3:10 PM the South Fork Dam broke. One witness described the noise as a "roaring like a mighty battle." Twenty million tons of water surged down the Conemaugh Valley with a force equal to that of the water plunging over Niagara Falls. It stripped the valley walls to the bare rock, scouring away trees, soil, boulders, and every living thing in its path. In a little over half an hour Lake Conemaugh was empty, its prized game fish flapping in the mud.

The monster that descended upon Johnstown changed shape and speed as it careened through the valley. At some points it was 40 feet (12 m) high, at others more than 80 feet (24 m). Where its momentum was checked by curves through a raceway of solid rock, the floodwater was slowed. But when the water had a straight downward grade, it accelerated. As it barreled downward, it picked up more and more debris. The water pushed trees, stones, and other solid matter like the shovel of a bulldozer into a great tangled mass. Many survivors would report that at first they did not see the water at all; just a moving pile of trash the size of a mountain.

South Fork was the first community to be hit. Fortunately, most of the village was built high up on the mountainside and out of reach. Only three people were killed and a handful of buildings destroyed. But one of them was the railway station. Now the thundering pile of wreckage included a caboose, four railway cars and a tangle of twisted steel rails.

Below South Fork, a narrow canyon and an ox-bow loop in the passage slowed the water's descent. Then its progress was momentarily stopped when the great mound of debris piled up against a stone viaduct. But only momentarily! As the angry waters surged back and forth, the masonry crumbled under the pressure and the viaduct crashed down.

With renewed fury the monster fell upon the hamlet of Mineral Point and obliterated it. Sixteen people who hadn't fled for their lives were killed. Several others found themselves in a wild ride down the river on the roofs of their houses.

East Conemaugh was next. People there had a two-minute warning thanks to engineer John Hess, who came down the line in his locomotive just ahead of the flood with his whistle shrieking. That alarm signal saved some lives, but not all. There were three passenger trains parked on sidings, and not everyone had a chance to get out.

The juggernaut smashed into the rail yard and scattered locomotives, some of them weighing 80 tons. At least twenty-eight local citizens were killed. No one knew how many train passengers died.

Now the flood had a straight downhill run and it picked up speed. It slammed into Woodvale, a small community on the outskirts of Johnstown. By the time the brown water had rushed past, only one building in Woodvale was left standing. More than 300 people were dead. A factory that manufactured barbed wire was destroyed, adding miles of the slashing, strangling wire to the already lethal mass of wreckage. Now it was Johnstown's turn. The time was about 4:07.

Some survivors would say that the first sign they had of something amiss was a sudden gust of wind that pressed them against buildings. Others said it was "a roar, like thunder." Many claimed that it was the appearance in the air above roofs and trees of a black cloud of dust and spray – a "death mist."

The monster rolled through Johnstown like a threshing machine through a field of wheat. Houses, railroad cars, trees, horses, and people vanished in the maelstrom of wreckage and brown foam. The advance wave struck a hill on the far side of the Stony Creek River, causing a huge backwash to surge over Johnstown, smashing anything that had withstood the first onslaught. With its velocity somewhat diminished, the wave threw its vanguard of rubbish up against a stone bridge that spanned the Conemaugh River just below the point where the Little Conemaugh and the Stony Creek met.

Once again the tons of debris formed a dam. This time the bridge held. A lake of filthy water now covered the ground upon which Johnstown sat.

Horace Rose had just passed the coffee across to his neighbor when he heard the first loud rumble. He ran up to the third floor and looked out.

Coming straight at his house was a 35-foot (10.6 m) high wall of tumbling debris. The thing was grinding down all in its path. One of Rose's sons was at his side. The boy cried, "Can we escape?" Rose quietly replied, "No, this means death to us all." Seconds later he was plunged into darkness.

When Rose awoke, he was pinned under fallen timbers. He was in agony, with his right ribs, shoulder, and arm crushed. He heard one of his sons cry for help, but was unable to go to him. His daughter, June, popped up out of the water, then went down again. Rose couldn't see his wife, Maggie.

Then a man named Phillips emerged from the swirling water. He found Maggie and freed her from the timbers that had collapsed on her. Someone – possibly Phillips – pulled June to the surface. Soon Horace, Maggie, June, and Forest, along with several other survivors were on a floating roof. There was no sign of Percy or Winter.

The roof drifted for hours before it finally bumped into a hotel that had remained intact. The survivors climbed in through an upper window and spent a night of cold misery huddled in the darkness. Horace was in excruciating pain and was certain that his missing sons were dead. Winter and Percy would eventually be found alive and unhurt. Their neighbors were not so fortunate. Little Bessie Fronheiser and her mother both died.

When James Quinn went to the door with his cigar, he saw the black mist and heard the roar of approaching doom. He ran back into the house and shouted, "Run for your lives! Follow me straight to the hill! Don't go back for anything!"

He dashed up the stairs and came down with little Marie wrapped in a blanket. He rushed out the door with Rosemary and Helen clinging to his elbows. Behind him were Abbie, with her baby, and Libby Hipp, who carried Gertrude.

The hill James Quinn headed for wasn't far away, but the water was already up to the children's chins. He fought his way through it, with the girls clutching to his arms for dear life. When at last they had scrambled up the hillside to safety, James looked around and saw to his horror that the others were not right behind him. He started to go back, only to see his house collapse into the water.

Instead of following her brother-in-law, Abbie had taken Libby and the two children back into the house and up to the third floor. Then as Abbie prayed and Gertrude screamed, "Papa, Papa, Papa!" the house shook violently. The floorboards burst open, and the dirty water welled up from below. One moment Gertrude could see her aunt, baby cousin, and nursemaid; the next, they were gone.

Gertrude spat out the "horrible water" and struggled to keep her head above the surface. She somehow managed to crawl out through a hole in the smashed house and onto a floating mattress. All of her clothes had been torn off except her underwear.

Gertrude almost fell off the mattress when it collided with a dead horse. She called out for help to a man on the roof of a house that floated by. He either didn't hear her, or ignored her. Then a roof with about twenty people on it drifted near. Gertrude again cried for help.

One man stood up and started for the edge, but others tried to hold him back. He fought them off and plunged into the water. As Gertrude screamed for him to save her, his head kept disappearing and then surfacing again. Finally, he pulled himself onto the mattress. Gertrude wrapped her arms around him tightly and wouldn't let go. They watched as the big roof he had just abandoned was sucked down by a whirlpool.

The man who had come to Gertrude's rescue was Maxwell McAchren. Even though he had succeeded in reaching the child, he didn't know how he was going to take her to safety. They were entirely at the mercy of the wind and the current.

Then the mattress drifted near a house perched on a hillside. It was only 15 or 20 feet (4.5 or 6 m) away, but McAchren had no way to move in closer. Two men leaned out of a window and tried unsuccessfully to reach the mattress with long poles. Then one of them called to McAchren, "Throw that baby over here!"

McAchren shouted back, "Do you think you can catch her?"

The man replied, "We can try."

One man hung out the window, with his companion clutching his legs. McAchren picked Gertrude up and tossed her across the water. The terrified little girl landed right in the dangling man's arms.

The men wrapped Gertrude in a warm, dry blanket. Later she was taken to a house that was crowded with other refugees of the flood, and put to bed. Nobody knew who the child was, and she was too traumatized by her ordeal to speak. It would be the following day before someone recognized her and told James Quinn that his daughter was alive. Maxwell McAchren was rescued when some men hauled his mattress ashore with ropes.

Victor Heiser had just freed the horses and was at the doorway of the barn when he heard the frightful roar. He looked across the flooded yard and saw his father at an upstairs window. George was frantically signaling to him to go back inside and climb to the loft. The teenager did so, and then went through a trapdoor to the roof. From there he could see the vast wall of wreckage bearing down on him. Before Victor's eyes his home was pulverized with his parents in it.

The barn was torn loose and began to roll. Stumbling and grabbing at anything that he could hold onto, Victor managed to stay on whichever part of the barn was on top. Then it smashed into the side of a house. Victor leapt onto that building's roof, only to find it collapsing under him. He grabbed at the eaves of yet another building that had crashed into it, and hung there by his fingertips.

Victor couldn't pull himself up, and pain from his hands was shooting into his arms. Finally he could hold on no longer, and fell. He landed hard on a piece of roof from the barn.

Now Victor was riding across the ruins of Johnstown on a rolling, heaving expanse of water. He saw a house with a family he knew well clinging to the roof. It was crushed under tons of wreckage. His own raft was carried in amongst the deadly piles of debris. Victor had to dodge falling logs and other pieces of junk, while trying to stay on the roof. He narrowly escaped being crushed by a railway car that came hurtling down. Finally he drifted close to

Dozens of displaced buildings and tons of debris brought desolation to Johnstown. Survivors gathered on rooftops the day after the flood to survey the devastation.

a brick house that was still standing. Victor climbed onto the roof, which was already occupied by several shivering survivors. It had been but ten minutes since his home had been demolished.

The shattered buildings of Johnstown added to the huge mass of debris the current was washing toward the jam-up at the bridge. The flotsam included houses and toys, furniture and trees, drowned dogs and horses, and human beings both living and dead. Somehow the massive dam at the bridge caught fire.

No one was certain what started the blaze. Wreckage could have been covered with spilled oil from any one of a number of sources. Perhaps one of the houses that had been carried to the jam-up had a coal stove in which the fire had not been doused. Whatever the origin, flames were soon racing through the jumble of trees and broken timber. From 500 to 600 people were trapped in the wreckage. Throughout the night and the next day rescue workers, Victor Heiser among them, struggled to get them out. But with few tools available, the rescuers could not reach everybody. At least eighty people were burned to death.

Downstream at Sang Hollow people did not know what was happening in Johnstown until the first bits of wreckage appeared on the river. Then through the spilling rain they saw people clinging to telegraph poles and pieces of houses. Bill Heppenstall and the other passengers poured out of the stalled train and rushed to the riverbank. They watched helplessly as the victims hurtled past. Then a house became entangled in overhanging trees. From it came the cries of a baby.

Without hesitation, 17-year-old Bill said he was going after the child. Other people told him it was impossible, but the teenager ignored them. He tore the

The raging floodwaters snapped large trees like sticks and turned them into battering rams that could pierce walls. This house was skewered by a huge tree, and then dumped in a new location. Miraculously, the inhabitants all came out alive.

bell cord out of a passenger car, tied it around his body and dove into the furious water. While men on the riverbank held onto this lifeline, Bill swam out to the house. He soon returned with the baby. While the crowd was cheering him, Bill said that the mother was still out there, and he was going back for her. He took along a railroad tie to help hold her up. Bill rescued the mother just before the house was torn loose from the trees and borne away on the angry waters.

The flood took only ten minutes to ravage Johnstown. The number of dead was undoubtedly higher than the official count of 2,209. Among them were 396 children. Another ninety-eight children had lost both parents. Ninety-six whole families had been wiped out.

The days following the calamity were extremely difficult for the survivors. Flood conditions hampered the arrival of assistance from outside the mountain town. Hundreds of survivors had lost everything but the clothes on their backs, and some didn't even have that. There was little food and almost no medical supplies for the injured. There was no water. The filthy muck that lapped the hillsides where people had sought refuge was fouled by garbage and the waste from outdoor privies. Bobbing on the surface or trapped underneath were human bodies and the corpses of domestic animals and rats. It would be months before the body of the last flood victim would be found. The remains of hundreds could not be identified.

The Johnstown survivors rebuilt their town, and as best they could, their lives. Many, like the Quinns, stayed in Johnstown. Three years after the flood, Horace Rose officiated at the dedication of a monument to 777 unknown victims.

Others, like Victor Heiser, left. With his parents dead and his home destroyed, Victor had nothing to keep him in Johnstown. He went to medical school and earned international fame for developing a treatment for leprosy that saved millions of lives. But for the rest of his life Victor would be haunted by nightmares about that horrifying day when he had been a lone, frightened boy caught in the terrors of the Johnstown Flood.

The management of the South Fork Hunting and Fishing Club, and the members who were present on May 31, made a hasty departure when the dam broke. Not one of them went down to the valley to help out when every able-bodied man was needed. Considering that they were all millionaires, the donations a few of them made to relief funds were paltry indeed. There were official inquiries and numerous lawsuits, but no one associated with the Club was ever made accountable for the disaster. There were definitely advantages to being rich and powerful.

3

· · · — — · · ·

THE SPRINGHILL MINE
DISASTER OF 1891
TERROR UNDERGROUND

oal mining in the late nineteenth century was extremely dangerous. Mines could cave in or flood, and there were frequent accidents with explosive materials. By February of 1891, the mine at Springhill, Nova Scotia had already claimed the lives of twenty miners. One especially deadly hazard was the gas that came off coal. The lighter-than-air coal gas, called firedamp, generally rose out of the mine through ventilation shafts. But sometimes gas was trapped in pockets or cavities. Firedamp was highly combustible. Even the friction from a miner's drill was enough to ignite the volatile fumes. Then the exploding gas would set fire to the coal dust that always filled the air in the passageways. After the firedamp burned, it left behind three kinds of poisonous gases: "after damp" and "black damp," both heavier than air; and "white damp," which was lighter than air, odorless, and colorless. A person might survive an encounter with after damp or black damp. But one breath of white damp was fatal.

~~~

At 7 o'clock on the morning of February 21, 1891, Danny Robertson was among the crowd of workers descending the steep slope into the Cumberland Railway and Coal Company mine at Springhill. Danny was a driver. His job was to handle a pit pony named Jenny that pulled a train, or rake, of coal cars through the gloomy tunnels hundreds of feet underground. Like the miners who rode down into the mine with him in one of those rakes, Danny wore a hat equipped with a small oil lamp to light his way. His hands were calloused from hard work, and his fingernails were constantly black from coal dust. The sun had not yet come up when Danny entered the mine, and it would be well after sunset when he finished his shift. Miners called that "working from can't see to can't see." Danny Robertson was 14 years old.

Danny wasn't the only boy heading down into the black pit that morning, nor was he the youngest. Jon Conway, a driver like Danny, was 13. Willie Terris was just 12. He was a trapper, one of the boys who spent long hours sitting on a chair, opening and closing the ventilation doors, called traps, that linked one tunnel to another. So was Willard Carter. That day was actually Willard's 13th birthday. His job was important because the traps let gas out and fresh air in. But it was also extremely monotonous and he looked forward to the time when he could be promoted from trapper to miner.

In mining towns like Springfield, boys left school at an early age to work for the colliery. The company employed boys for a variety of menial tasks. In addition to feeding and driving the pit ponies and working the traps, they loaded coal, cleaned lamps, and packed gunpowder cans. When they had grown big enough, they went to work at the coalface as miners, just like their fathers. Putting boys to work was considered good economics for the mine owners. They paid the youngsters substantially less than they paid the men, thus increasing company profits. The boys' earnings were important to their families' incomes, because even their fathers were not very well paid.

And so lads like Tom Davis, 15, Jim Johnson, 16, George Martin, 14, and Murdoch and Philip Ross, 14 and 16, pulled on their pit boots every morning and went down to toil in the mine, For many of them, that cold February dawn would be their last. Death awaited them underground.

The Springfield mine was one of the biggest coal producers in Canada, turning out more than 2,000 tons a day. It was also reputed to be among the safest. Pumps kept it dry and the trappers kept the air moving. At the insistence of the Miner's Union, inspectors regularly checked the tunnels for gas. Only two days before, Underground Manager James Conway had made an inspection and pronounced the mine clean.

Deep underground, young boys like this one toiled long days loading coal, driving pit ponies and working the ventilation shafts. Families needed the extra money the boys brought home. But thirty teenage boys never returned home after a deadly explosion ripped through the Springhill mine.

The men and boys worked from 7:00 AM until noon, when they stopped for lunch. Bits of sandwiches dirtied by coal-blackened fingers were tossed to the waiting rats. At 12:30 everybody resumed work. Thirteen minutes later, an explosion ripped through the mine.

In just a few terrifying seconds the ignited gas did its lethal work. First a rush of wind swept through the mine like a tornado, tearing through trap doors as if they were paper, and carrying clouds of dust, timbers, and other debris. The wind was instantly followed by a barrage of fireballs, both large and small, that rocketed down the passageways like roman candles. Then a mass of flame filled tunnels and roasted everything and everyone in its path. As the coal dust burned, it unleashed a creeping, murderous ghost of white damp into those parts of the mine untouched by fire. The poisonous gas hunted down men and boys trying to escape.

Danny Robertson was on the front of a rake, driving Jenny up a slope when the blast of searing air hit him hard enough to throw him right back into an empty coal car. At the same instant, Willie Terris saw a flash of fire coming straight at him. He dove under his chair and buried his face in his hands.

Moments later, Danny sat up in the coal car somewhat dazed. From up and down the tunnel he could hear the crash of falling coal and timbers. The lamp in his cap had been blown out, but he was not in complete darkness. His clothes were burning and by the dim glow he could see that Jenny was dead. Danny tore off his flaming coat and vest and discovered that his hands and arms were badly burned. In terrible pain, and with no light at all to guide him now, he began to grope his way through the pitch-black tunnel.

As Danny stumbled along, his heart racing with fear, he heard a boyish whimper; a weak cry for help. In spite of his injuries and his fright, Danny groped his way toward the sound. He found Willie cringing under his chair. The child had been only slightly burned on his ears and the backs of his hands, but was paralyzed with fear.

Danny's hands and arms were too badly burned for him to pick Willie up and carry him, so he persuaded the boy to climb onto his back. All the way up the long tunnel, Danny carried Willie piggyback, afraid that at any moment another explosion could blow them to kingdom come. As they approached the mine entrance, they met rescue workers who were already heading down. The men wrapped Willie in a blanket to take him home, but Danny wasn't quite ready to be rescued himself. He had an older brother who also worked in the mine, and the first thing the boy asked was if his brother was safe. When the men said that they didn't know, Danny started to turn around to go back. The men stopped him and sent him the rest of the way to the surface in a rake full of injured miners. One of them, it turned out, was Danny's brother, wounded but alive. Outside, someone offered to take Danny home on a sled, but the young hero insisted upon walking home. He said that he didn't want to alarm his mother.

Daniel Beaton, 13, also owed his life to a heroic act. He was badly burned, and had been struck on the head by a flying missile that tore off his scalp and left his skull exposed. His 17-year-old brother, John, had been working nearby. After the explosion, John, who had not been badly hurt, hurried to where Daniel was supposed to be, but couldn't find his brother. With no thought for his own safety he searched for Daniel until he found him. When other miners met John, he was carrying the wounded boy in his arms.

It took but fifteen minutes for people on the surface to organize rescue operations. Many of the men and boys who'd been down in the pit had been far enough away from the explosion to escape the worst of the blast, and had been quick enough to get out before the gas reached them. But approximately 150 men and boys were still missing. One was John Conway, whose father, James, had inspected the mine and declared it clean. James was at a meeting above ground when the accident occurred. He was one of the first to go down to look for survivors.

As crowds of frantic wives and mothers gathered at the mine entrance, miners and other volunteers crawled through rubble in the black pit. They had wet cloths across their faces to protect them from gas. Even so, at places their advance was slowed by the presence of noxious fumes.

As their lamps pierced the gloom, the glow revealed scenes of utter horror. Bodies were sprawled everywhere. Some were burned beyond recognition. A few had no heads. Others had not a mark on them, but were coated with a layer of ash that made them look like grey statues. Some of the victims who had been asphyxiated by gas appeared simply to have gone to sleep, unaware that they were dying. The faces of others were contorted from their final struggles to breathe.

One searcher, Jesse Armishaw, found his two sons dead. The two Ross boys, Murdoch and Philip, were dead. Eerily, one of them was still standing, his arm propping him up against some support. Another man was held upright by rubble piled up to his waist.

James and David McVey, 14 and 16, were discovered poisoned, clasped in each other's arms. Adolphus Landry, 14, was found pinned beneath a dead horse, severely burned but alive. Willard Carter's trap had been completely demolished, and he was injured. The boy who had entered his teens that very day would live to enjoy future birthdays. Adolphus and Willard were among the pitifully few wounded to be taken out.

As the crowd at the mine entrance watched in grim silence, the rescue parties emerged into the cold daylight. Occasionally they bore a wounded victim. More often a man staggered out with a body on his back and his lamp clenched in his teeth. One of them was Oliver Dupee, who carried the body of his son, Joseph. Fate was especially cruel to the Dupee family that day. As Mr. Dupee approached his house with Joseph in his arms, his four-year-old son ran out. The child slipped on the ice and struck his head so hard on the frozen ground that he died.

Down in the pit, after an hour of finding nothing but more bodies, the searchers were certain they would find no one else alive. They were about to return to the surface, when they heard a faint cry of "Mother!" Following the direction of the sound, the men found Joseph Conway pinned under a dead horse. The boy was only slightly hurt. The very fact that he was alive was considered a miracle.

Including those who would die from their injuries, the total death toll for the Springhill mine disaster of 1891 was 125. Thirty of the dead were teenagers. Seventeen of them were boys 16 or younger. Economic need had snatched childhood from them too soon. And then it had taken away the promise of manhood.

An enquiry found that no one was to blame for the disaster. The accident had evidently been caused by a gunpowder charge set off to loosen coal from the face of a seam. Ordinarily, packing around the explosive material prevented any flame from escaping into the mine. This time there was an unusual crack in the coalface that allowed the charge to ignite gas and dust that had probably accumulated during the lunch break. That explanation, at least, was the conclusion reached by the inquiry. The three miners who had set the charge had all been killed.

After the dead had been buried and the mine reopened, there were recommendations for improved safety. New equipment was installed to remove gas, inspections would be made after meal breaks, and gunpowder would be banned in areas where dust was heavy. But many years would pass before companies were forbidden by law to exploit adolescent workers, and wages improved so that families would not have to depend upon the toil of their children. Today in the town of Springhill a white monument of a coal miner stands in memory of the men and boys who lost their lives on that day of terror underground.

4

· · · — — · · ·

MONT PELÉE
"THE VOLCANO IS COMING!"

The island of Martinique is about 400 square miles (1,036 sq km) in area and lies in the crescent of small Caribbean islands called the Lesser Antilles. Much of the interior is rugged, making travel difficult. In 1902 most transportation between coastal communities was still by sea. Mont Pelée, rising to 4,430 feet (1,350 m), dominates the northern end of the island. Just four miles (6.4 km) from the mountain's base, the city of St. Pierre overlooked a beautiful bay.

By the turn of the twentieth century the island's principal exports – sugar, rum and bananas – had fueled St. Pierre's growth into a prosperous city of over 25,000, larger than the capital, Fort-du-France, which had about 17,500 residents. It was a paradise, with the best of the technological and natural worlds. Electricity lit its streets and powered the tram cars that carried people to and from their jobs. Society people dined in fine French restaurants and enjoyed theatrical productions. The more adventurous would climb up Pelée's forested slopes for picnics. Some even swam in the lake in one of the volcano's two large craters.

Everybody knew that Pelée had erupted in the past and that people had been killed. But those eruptions had not been catastrophic, and the mountain had been quiet for almost fifty years. Most people in St. Pierre and the surrounding villages believed that the volcano was dormant. They did not understand that the passing of a generation in human terms is but a tick of the second-hand in geological time.

~~~

Just after 7:00 on the morning of May 8, 1902, the ferryboat *Diamant* sailed into the port of St. Pierre, Martinique. As dawn broke over the Caribbean island, young Jean-Baptiste Innocent, the ship's boy, could see what the ship's passengers had come to look at – the smoke-shrouded volcano, Mont Pelée that towered above the city. For almost two weeks the mountain had been rumbling and belching out clouds of smoke, accompanied by showers of ash. On that Ascension Thursday, a holiday in the largely Catholic French colony, many residents of the capital, Fort-du-France, 11 miles (17.7 km) by sea to the south, had taken advantage of a day off work to see the spectacle up close.

As the *Diamant* chugged its way to the wharf past seventeen or eighteen large vessels riding at anchor, and countless fishing boats and other small craft, the ship's boy on an Italian ship, the *Teresa Lo Vico* went about his duties just as Jean-Baptiste was doing. Before an hour would pass, the two lads would share something besides their humble rank in a ship's crew.

The steamer *Roraima* of the Quebec Line also sailed into St. Pierre that morning. Among its passengers were Mrs. Clement Stokes, a widow from New York, her children Rita, 9, Eric, 4, and a baby girl, and their young Barbadian nurse, Clara King. The *Roraima's* skipper, Captain George Muggah, told Mrs. Stokes that he did not intend to remain in port any longer than was absolutely necessary.

In the city, the bells of St. Pierre Cathedral called parishioners to Mass. Young Haviva Da Ilfrile was in church with her mother, as was the family of plantation owner Edouard Lasserre. Lasserre's daughter Hélène was to celebrate her first communion, but as the service began, Lasserre received an urgent message concerning his livestock. He rushed out of town, leaving Hélène and the rest of his family in the cathedral.

Not all in the city went to church that morning. In one house an unidentified man and a little girl with a blue ribbon in her hair – probably father and daughter – sat down to breakfast like many others. Planter Fernand Clerc, one of the most important men in the colony was not in church either. He bundled his wife and children into a carriage and whipped his team to a gallop. He was taking his family to what he hoped would be the safety of their country house about three miles (5 km) out of town. He had decided that morning that the mountain had given them warnings enough. Clerc had wanted the town evacuated. So had Professor Gaston Landes, perhaps the most highly educated man in the colony. But nobody had listened to the two men. Now, Clerc fled with his family. He was afraid that the mountain would erupt at any moment and wreak devastation on St. Pierre. He was right.

When the mountain had begun to spew out smoke and ash late in April, few people were alarmed. As a layer of white ash settled on St. Pierre, children played in it, pretending it was snow. Martinique's governor, Louis Mouttet, assured the population that all was well. Andreus Hurrard, editor of St. Pierre's newspaper, *Les Colonies,* told his readers that there was no danger. In fact, nobody on the island knew much about volcanoes, including Professor Landes. He had advised evacuating the city, as had M. Clerc, but he could not say specifically what the mountain might do. Everybody thought that if Pelée *did* erupt, it would send out lava flows that would follow ravines down the mountainside to the sea. People would just have to stay out of the lava's path. When the little rivers flowing down from the mountain suddenly became raging torrents, everyone was completely baffled. No one knew that volcanic activity was forcing water from subterranean streams and reservoirs to the surface.

As the days went by and Pelée continued to belch and thunder, a few people left St. Pierre. But the little city's population was swollen by frightened villagers, who poured in from the countryside. Along with the country people came hordes of rats, snakes and centipedes, fleeing the smoke and shaky ground of Pelée's upper slopes. Snakebites and centipede stings became a serious problem in what would be St. Pierre's last days.

In the first week of May, Mont Pelée's volcanic activity continued intermittently. The mountain would blow rocks high into the sky, and then seem to settle down for a while. On May 5, a gigantic slide of boiling mud composed of saturated volcanic ash suddenly rolled down the mountainside, destroying everything in its path. This steaming avalanche engulfed a sugar mill, killing more than 150 workmen. But the fact that the mudslide followed the course of a ravine reinforced the belief that a lava flow would do the same thing. Then came news of a devastating volcanic eruption on the British island of St. Vincent, 90 miles (145 km) to the south of Martinique. Hundreds were killed in that tragedy. But though the people of St. Pierre sympathized with the victims on St. Vincent, they also felt relief. Surely, they thought, the blast on St. Vincent would have reduced the pressures that were boiling up in Mont Pelée. Only eighteen hours after the St. Vincent eruption, they would learn – too late – how wrong they were.

A few minutes after 8:00 AM on May 8, Mont Pelée did more than erupt. It exploded! The volcano's cone shot a huge cloud of steam and ash seven miles (11 km) into the atmosphere. At the same time the side of the mountain blew out and discharged the dragon that would annihilate St. Pierre – *nuée ardente,* a vast, superheated cloud of steam, ash, and exploding gases heavier than air, that rolled down the side of a volcano with frightening speed!

Racing down the mountainside at 120 mph (193 kph), the nuée ardente took only two minutes to reach St. Pierre and smother it in a billowing white-hot mass. For the 35,000 men, women and children in the city there was no time to run and no place to hide. Under the cover of a sinister black cloud laced with lightning flashes, they died en masse. People in the streets were slammed to the ground by the shockwave that preceded the inferno. Those who were indoors were crushed under the rubble of collapsing buildings. For any who survived the first assault, there was still no escape. It took but one breath of the burning gas to sear throats and lungs. Volcanic steam enveloped people and cooked them alive inside their own skins, sometimes leaving not a visible mark of violence.

As fires burst out across the city, other victims were burned so completely that they no longer resembled human beings. The victims in the middle of the holocaust were the lucky ones because they died instantly. Scores of people on the outer fringes would take hours or even days to die from agonizing burns or inhalation of deadly gas.

While the tail of the dragon was still slithering down the mountain, its maw swallowed up St. Pierre's waterfront and everything in it. Thousands of barrels of rum in warehouses and on the docks exploded, sending a deluge of liquid fire into the bay. Every ship and small vessel was either capsized or set ablaze. Only one ship, the British freighter *Roddam,* badly damaged and with just a few horribly burned members of her crew still alive, remained afloat.

Fernand Clerc and his family had abandoned their carriage on the road and run up a hill overlooking St. Pierre. They had escaped in the nick of time. Now they witnessed the total destruction of St. Pierre. Clerc's wife Véronique said later: "We saw a sea of fire cutting through the billowing black smoke and advancing along the ground toward the town. What could we do? We held each other close. St. Pierre was doomed. Our friends were doomed. Our world was doomed."

Fernand Clerc added: "It grew so dark that I could only be sure of the presence of my wife and children by groping for them and touching them with my hands."

Clerc was fortunate to have saved his family. Edouard Lasserre, in a carriage with his driver and plantation manager, had just reached the hills outside of town when the force of the blast threw men, horses, and carriage right off the road. The animals were killed, but the three men, though badly burned, were alive. Back in the cathedral little Hélène Lasserre and everyone else who had gone to church were dead. All but one.

Haviva Da Ilfrile had left the church, sent by her mother

The once-beautiful city of St. Pierre, the Paris of the Caribbean, lay in smoldering ruins after the eruption of Mt. Pelée in 1902. Only one person who had been in the city at the time survived. He was locked within the thick walls of the city's prison. Thirty thousand law-abiding citizens were not so lucky.

on an errand to her aunt's house, near a place called the Corkscrew, an old crater near the edge of town. She later gave a vivid account of those horrifying moments:

"I had hardly gone more than three steps when I felt a hot wind from the Corkscrew. Thinking that something must be on fire, I ran to the top of the path, and there I saw the bottom of the pit all red, like boiling, with little blue flames shooting up from it. There were two guides leading a woman up the path and hurrying as fast as they could run. I saw a puff of blue smoke seem to hit the party, and they fell as if killed."

Haviva ran for her life toward the waterfront.

"Just as I got to the main street, I saw this boiling stuff burst from the top of the Corkscrew and run down the side of the hill. It followed the road first, but then, as the stream got bigger, it ate up the houses on both sides of the road. Then I saw that a boiling red river was coming from another part of the hill and cutting off the escape of the people who were running out of the houses."

Haviva reached the waterfront and found her brother's boat tied to a pier. She untied it and jumped in, then looked around as she heard a cry. She saw her brother racing toward the pier.

"But he was too late, and I heard him scream as the stream first touched him and then swallowed him."

Haviva wrapped herself in a canvas. Her little boat was blown out to sea, but somehow she managed to paddle it to a small cave where she had often played with her friends.

"But before I got there, I looked back – and the whole side of the mountain which was near the town seemed to open and boil down on the screaming people. I was burned a good deal by the stones and ashes that came flying about the boat, but I got to the cave."

French sailors found Haviva there several days later. Sadly, she died shortly after from her injuries.

On the *Roraima* Clara King, the nursemaid, was helping Mrs. Stokes get the children dressed for breakfast when they heard the steward shout, "Close the cabin door! The volcano is coming!" No sooner had the door been slammed shut than everyone was thrown to the deck as the explosion rocked the ship. Clara quickly gathered Rita and Eric into her arms while Mrs. Stokes clung to her baby. Then a skylight burst open and a shower of hot, moist ash poured in on them, covering everyone in a scalding blanket.

The *Roraima* was in flames and many of her crew, including Captain Muggah, were dead. But a few of the men had survived. The first engineer broke into the Stokes' cabin and dragged everyone out. The baby was already dead. Little Eric, who'd had all of his hair and clothing burned off, died as the sailors tenderly wrapped him in a blanket. Mrs. Stokes, too, was dying. Her last words were to tell Clara to take Rita to her aunt. Rita and Clara, though seriously burned, survived. They and the few remaining sailors huddled on the forward section of the wrecked ship for almost seven hours before being rescued.

Jean-Baptiste Innocent was on the wharf, having just helped the last of the passengers disembark, when the whole world seemed to erupt in thunder and fire. The *Diamant* capsized and her boiler exploded. Jean-Baptiste dove into the water and stayed under until he could no longer hold his breath. When he surfaced, he saw that the entire waterfront was ablaze. Jean-Baptiste clung to a floating plank for seven hours before he was rescued. All of the passengers who had come from Fort-du-France to see the volcano up close were dead. Jean-Baptiste was the only member of the *Diamant's* crew to survive.

As soon as the ship's boy on the *Teresa Lo Vico* felt the heat from the explosion, he dropped to his hands and knees and stuck his head in a bucket of water. That action may well have saved the youngster from disfigurement, perhaps even death. Then, with the ship in flames and sinking, the engineer and the boy managed to launch a lifeboat and rescue nine other sailors and three women.

The blast was heard all the way to Fort-du-France, and when the telegraph line from St. Pierre went dead in the same instant, people in the capital knew that something terrible had happened. The French naval cruiser *Suchet* was dispatched to St. Pierre, and her crew rescued as many people as they could from the chaos in the bay. But the heat from the hell that had been St. Pierre was so intense that two days passed before anyone could venture into the ruins.

St. Pierre was now a city of the dead. The stench of sulfur and burned flesh was everywhere. Professor Landes was dead, along with newspaper editor Andreus Hurrard. So were Governor Mouttet and his wife, who had gone to St. Pierre from their residence in Fort-du-France the day before the eruption to assure the population that there was no danger. The military men and police who had the awful task of cremating human remains to prevent disease walked through scenes out of a nightmare. In one place they found the charred bodies of nine children, all embracing each other. In another they found some girls whose bodies had been burned to a crisp, but whose shoes were inexplicably undamaged. In the rubble of one house, slumped over the table as though asleep, untouched by fire, were the bodies of a man and a little girl with a blue ribbon in her hair.

Unbelievably, there was one survivor in St. Pierre. A young man named Auguste Ciparis had been locked in solitary confinement in the St. Pierre jail when Pelée hurled its killer cloud upon the city. The thick walls of the cell had protected him from the blast and the intense heat. Ciparis had been burned by hot ash that came through his tiny window. He endured three days of pain, thirst, and hunger before he was discovered. So astonishing was Ciparis' survival, that he became a star attraction in Barnum and Baily's Circus. The story circulated that he was a condemned murderer, scheduled to be executed the very morning Pelée blew. The less-colorful truth was that he had been jailed for public drunkenness and assault.

Because St. Pierre had been jammed with refugees from the countryside, no one would ever know how many people died that morning. Thirty thousand was the "official" estimate. Though a small community was eventually built amidst the ruins, St. Pierre never did rise again. The dust of the graceful little city lies forever buried with the ashes of its people.

In the aftermath of the disaster, Governor Mouttet and editor Hurrard – especially Mouttet – would be vilified and held responsible for the stunning loss of life. By then both men were conveniently dead and could not defend their actions. Though they had made bad judgments in assuring the population that all was well, in all likelihood they did so out of a lack of scientific knowledge rather than incompetence or stupidity, as their accusers would charge.

The nuée ardente *(glowing cloud) is something that modern volcanologists call a pyroclastic surge. Early twentieth-century scientists were not familiar with this kind of eruption. After the horrific demonstration given by Mont Pelée on the island of Martinique, they would call the phenomenon Peléan.*

5

· · · — — · · ·

THE FRANK SLIDE
THE NIGHT THE
MOUNTAIN WALKED

The town of Frank, in what is now the Canadian province of Alberta, was barely two years old in the spring of 1903. It owed its existence to a rich deposit of high quality coal in the bowels of Turtle Mountain, which loomed above the little community. In the early twentieth century, coal was the fuel that heated homes, drove ships and trains, and powered the machinery of industry. But a shadow hung over the coal-mining town – literally! Turtle Mountain rose 7,200 feet (2,194 m) above the junction of Gold Creek and the Old Man River, where Frank was built. Protruding from the mountainside, about 2,300 feet (700 m) above the town was a massive outcropping of limestone that gave the mountain its name. This giant "turtle's head" was 2,100 feet (640 m) wide, 3,000 feet (914 m) high, and 500 feet (152 m) thick. Sometimes the ground around Turtle Mountain shook. Cree, Blackfoot, and Crow Natives called it "The Mountain That Walks," and stayed away from it. Native legend predicted that one day the giant turtle would shake its head and hurl destruction down upon anyone foolish enough to be at its feet. For eons it had withstood the relentless levelers of great mountains: the elements and gravity. But now man was hacking away at the mountain's heart, hauling out a thousand tons of coal a day.

~~~

Fifteen-year-old Lillian Clark had never spent a night away from home in her life. On the night of April 28, 1903, however, she had worked late at her job as a maid at the miners' boarding house in Frank. She decided to spend the night, rather than walk back in the dark to her family's home on the other side of Gold Creek. In the Clark home, one of a row of seven frame bungalows on the very edge of town, slept Lillian's mother and five younger brothers and sisters: Charles, Albert, Alfred, Ellen, and Gertrude. Lillian's father, Alex, was with nineteen other miners working the night shift in the Frank coal mine. Lillian didn't know it as she drifted off to sleep in the boarding house, but she would never see any of her family again.

Miners like Lillian's father had flocked to the new town site, which had been named for the mine's owner, American banker H. L. Frank. They were followed by merchants and tradesmen, who set up shop along Frank's main street. The population had quickly grown to over 600.

Frank could be a rowdy place on Saturday nights, when local cowboys rode into town to drink in the saloons and brawl with the miners. But a detachment of North West Mounted Police kept order. The community had three churches, a schoolhouse, and a bank. Located just east of the Crowsnest Pass, right on the Canadian Pacific Railroad, Frank was a boomtown with all the promise of a bright future. But there had been portents of disaster. Native legend warned that one day Turtle Mountain would come crashing down. Coal meant money, however, and the newcomers – the white people – scoffed at what they considered Native superstition. Deep in the mountain the miners often felt tremors, but they became accustomed to them. These rumblings even made the miners' work easier because they shook the coal loose. All the men had to do was shovel it into pony carts for removal. Mining was a dangerous trade anywhere, and the men who did it accepted the hazards as part of the job. For the miners working in Turtle Mountain that night, a terrible nightmare was about to come true.

There had been a warm spell that April, with torrential rains that soaked the ground and sent rivers of water cascading down the mountainside. Then the temperature had dropped sharply. Water froze in the cracks and fissures of the great limestone wedge, and the ice began to expand.

A blizzard howled through the Crowsnest Pass, delaying a passenger train called the Spokane Flyer by an hour and a half. Fate was about to unleash a strange combination of spectacular luck and tragic loss on the unsuspecting people of Frank.

In the little row of houses across Gold Creek, other families besides Lillian Clark's had gone to bed. In one house slept Charles Ackroyd, his wife, Mary, and his 16-year-old stepson, Lester Johnston. Next door were Alex and Rosemary Leitch and their seven children. Their sons Athol, Wilfred, John, and Allen slept in one room, while daughters Jessie and Rosemary slept in another. Their five-month-old baby, Marion, was in bed between her parents. In her home nearby, Mrs. W. Warrington and her teenaged children Reginald, Florence, and Ivy were sleeping soundly, as was a visiting friend, Alex Dixon. The father of the family, Bill Warrington, was at work in the mine.

In the Bansemer household, Anne Bansemer was home with her children: Albert, Carl Jr., Frances, Rose, Hilda, Kate, and five-month-old Harold. Her husband, Carl, and two other sons were away. In yet another house, Sam and Lucy Ennis and their children Delbert, James, Hazel, and baby Gladys had long since retired. Elsewhere, railroad workers, off-duty miners, and men who were just passing through slept in barracks, the CPR livery stable, or whatever other accommodations they could find. A grizzled old trapper named Andy Gresack had bedded down in a tent pitched on the riverbank.

As midnight passed and the wee hours of April 29 moved toward dawn, not all of Frank slept. On a railway spur-line, engineer Ben Murgatroyd and brakemen Bill Lowes and Sid Choquette were shunting empty coal cars. In the town's electric light plant, Thomas Delap was the lone man on duty. In the saloons on the main street, a few customers were still drinking. And up above the town, in the belly of the mountain, the men of the night shift were digging away with picks and shovels. Shortly before 4:00 AM they stopped for lunch. Lillian Clark's father and two other men sat down to eat just outside the mine entrance, which was simply a big hole in the side of the mountain. Ten minutes later, exactly as the wary Natives had predicted, Turtle Mountain walked.

With a thundering roar that could be heard 15 miles (24 km) away, the gargantuan head of the turtle tore free of its age-old perch. Ninety million tons of limestone swept down the mountainside like an avalanche. The mass of shattered rock was so enormous, and its descent so swift, that it pushed a wall of cold, compressed air before it like a plow. This pocket-hurricane pulverized everything in its path – tents, wooden buildings, people. Many of the victims of the Frank Slide would have been dead even before they were hit by the rocks, which followed the air-blast by only scant seconds. Some of the rocks that plummeted down on Frank were as big as four-story houses. Others were no larger than baseballs, but fell in a deadly rain of millions.

Alex Clark and his two companions were the first to die that dreadful morning, as a storm of falling rock snatched them from their place at the mine entrance and buried them forever. In its wake, the landslide sealed the entrance and the ventilation shaft with tons of rubble. The seventeen surviving miners were now trapped inside Turtle Mountain.

Down in Frank, Ben Murgatroyd heard a sound like cannon fire. He looked up and saw a vision from hell coming right down on him and his men. Ben was a veteran engineer who was familiar with landslides in the Crowsnest Pass. He shouted for his brakemen to jump aboard and then rammed the throttle of his locomotive wide open. Sid Choquette and Bill Lowes jumped for the handrails as Ben's engine shot forward. Steel wheels shrieked on steel rails. The locomotive whipped across the bridge over Gold Creek like a bullet. No sooner had the train crossed the bridge, than the first wave of boulders smashed the structure to pieces.

The Frank Slide, the most disastrous recorded landslide in North American history, wreaked its havoc in about 100 seconds. In less than two minutes the promising future of Frank was destroyed forever and dozens of lives were snuffed out. The deadly wall of air and the thundering wave of rocks roared down into the valley below Turtle Mountain with such velocity that the debris spread a full 400 feet (122 m) up the opposite slope on a 2-mile (3.2-km) front. In its wake was desolation.

Andy Gresack, whose body was one of the few to be recovered, was dead in the shredded remains of his tent, with a frying pan still in his hand. The CPR livery stable, along with the horses and men who had been in it, was gone.

Amazingly, a puppy belonging to one of the miners who'd been sleeping there survived. The electric light plant and Thomas Delap were buried under a hundred feet of rock. A 2-mile (3.2-km) stretch of rails was either covered with rock or twisted like strands of spaghetti. Homes and barracks where people had been sleeping were no longer visible. A huge dam of fallen rock stretched across the Old Man River, causing the water to back up and form a lake. Over all hung a cloud of choking limestone dust.

Sid Choquette and Bill Lowes, the brakemen who had so narrowly escaped death, realized that the disaster could be followed by yet another if they did not act quickly. Somewhere up in the Crowsnest Pass the overdue Spokane Flyer would be racing toward Frank. In the pre-dawn darkness the engineer would not see the wall of rock across the railway until it was too late. The Flyer's crew and passengers were speeding toward certain death.

Lowes and Choquette scrambled across the wall of shattered limestone, hoping to reach the other side in time to flag the train down. It was a heroic act, because giant boulders continued to barrel down the mountainside. The rocks the men desperately stumbled over were sharp and still hot from friction. Lowes collapsed from exhaustion, but Choquette pushed on. By dead reckoning or sheer good luck, he scurried down the opposite side of the huge fan of rocks right at the spot where the tracks emerged. Choquette hurried along the line and was able to stop the Spokane Flyer. (Because Choquette had saved many lives, the CPR later rewarded him with a letter of commendation and $25.)

As dawn broke over the terrible scene, people from the unstricken parts of Frank were already swarming over the rocks in search of survivors. Some of those searchers would have been victims themselves but for sheer chance. One man and his visiting sister had decided to spend the night in the Frank hotel instead of the man's cabin. That cabin was now gone. Another man had declined an invitation to stay the night at a friend's house, because he had to go home to tend to his horses. The friend and all of his family were now dead under tons of rock.

One quarter of Frank had been demolished by the landslide. One of the most tragic points of devastation was that little row of houses on the other side of Gold Creek It would inaccurately be dubbed "Suicide Row." Yet, it was here that remarkable incidents of survival occurred.

Lillian Clark's mother and all of her brothers and sisters were dead. In the house next door the members of the Ennis family had suffered injuries – none of them life-threatening – but very nearly lost baby Gladys. As Mrs. Ennis lay in pain and shock from a broken collarbone, she heard the baby gagging. "Sam, Gladys is choking to death!" she cried to her husband. Help her if you can."

In spite of a broken hip, Sam found the baby. He scooped some mud out of her mouth with his fingers. Then he held her upside down and thumped her on the back until she coughed up more mud and was finally breathing normally.

Charles Ackroyd's house had been lifted right off its foundations when the wall of air hit. The last thing Lester Johnson would remember were the screams of his mother and stepfather – both of whom died. Then he lost consciousness. Lester awoke between two huge boulders, which ironically had protected him from the rock fall. He was in great pain, with a piece of broken board piercing his side. Lester was not even aware that he was stark naked. His pajamas had been completely torn from his body. He tried to move, but fainted from the excruciating pain. When he regained consciousness, Lester managed to break off the part of the board that was protruding from his side. He was in agony, but was able to crawl to Gold Creek and swim across. He made it to the home of Mr. and Mrs. Williams who were so astonished that the boy had emerged alive from the chaos of rock and shattered buildings that they seemed to not even notice that he was naked until Lester himself realized that he had no clothes on. Mrs. Williams examined the wound in Lester's side and found that feathers from his mattress or pillow had been jammed into it. She and her husband wrapped Lester in a blanket, put him in a wheelbarrow, and took him to the doctor.

The Bansemer family's house had been torn from its foundations and flipped over three times. Amazingly, the occupants crawled out of the wreckage practically unscathed. In the shattered Leitch house, however, rescuers found evidence of the quirky nature of fate. Jesse and Rosemary were alive, but the girls' parents and all of their brothers were dead. There was no sign of baby Marion. It did not seem possible that the infant could be alive.

Then came the most miraculous story of survival on that dreadful morning. As Mrs. Bansemer stumbled out of her wrecked house, she heard a baby cry. At the side of the building she found little Marion. The child had been

Lillian Clark, seen here at right as a younger girl, was the only member of her family to survive the Frank slide, the most disastrous landslide in North America's history.

thrown from her parents' bedroom and landed on a boulder that had come to rest against the Bansemer house. Unbelievably, a bale of hay from the CPR stable half a mile away had been deposited on the rock, cushioning the baby's fall. The little girl was unhurt.

Marion's incredible story would inspire a song, "The Ballad of Frankie Slide." It went, in part:

> *The baby girl lay on the rock*
> *'Twas a wonder she never died*
> *There was only one thing the folks could do*
> *They named her "Frankie Slide"*
> *They named her "Frankie Slide" they did*
> *There in the shiv'ring morning*

The ballad led to the myth that the baby was the sole survivor of the Frank Slide. In later years this story would be a cause of annoyance for Marion and the other survivors who had been "in the rocks." Only twenty-three of the people who had been in the path of the landslide escaped with their lives, and all had extraordinary tales to tell. One man told rescuers who were digging him out of the rubble to go carefully because he could feel something soft beneath him. When he was lifted out, the people found that there was indeed another person below him. A woman from the house next door had been thrown from her bed and somehow wound up under the man. She was badly injured, but alive.

While searchers were digging through the rubble looking for victims, another drama was being played out on the mountainside. Not knowing whether the men in the coal mine were dead or alive, rescuers were trying desperately to dig through to them. The North West Mounted Police had alerted the outside world by telegram, and soon miners from other communities were hurrying to the disaster area to help.

Inside the mine, the trapped men knew their chances didn't look good. The mountain could collapse on them at any moment. They could be poisoned by the gas that was an ever-present danger in coal mines. Or they could suffocate when the air supply ran out. Then, to their horror, they saw a new peril coming at them.

Water was now seeping into the mine as the river outside rose behind the stone dam. The entombed men knew if they stayed on the lower floor they would drown. But if they moved up to higher levels, they risked encountering the deadly, lighter-than-air gas. They worked frantically, trying to dig through the rubble that blocked their escape. But as fast as they shoveled debris out, more fell in. Their situation looked hopeless. Those who had families thought they would never see their wives and children again.

Things appeared just as grim to the workers outside. They tried digging and blasting to open the mine entrance and to make a breach in the dam, but to no effect. They did not give up, but even as they put their backs to the

A rescue team searching the Clark home the day after the slide found nothing but grim news. Lillian's mother and her five siblings had died in the slide. Lillian's father died, too, outside the mine where he was working, buried under ninety million tons of limestone.

work, they feared that they were fighting a losing battle. It seemed impossible to get through in time to save anyone who might still be alive.

But the men inside Turtle Mountain were experienced coal miners. They knew that seams of coal were exposed on the flanks of the mountain. They decided that their only hope was to hack a new tunnel right through the side of the mountain to the outside. Praying that it was the right place, they selected a spot and began to dig at an upward angle. They worked in relays as their muscles grew weary and the air became foul. It took thirteen hours of punishing toil for them to carve out a 36-foot (11-m) tunnel, but at last they broke through to daylight. As the exhausted miners sucked in clean, fresh air, one of them looked down and saw the small army of rescuers digging futilely at the mine entrance. He shouted to them, and within minutes men were hurrying up the slope to their aid. The trapped miners would see their families again after all.

But not Bill Warrington! Because he had an injured leg, Bill was the first man to be lifted out of the hole. When he looked down at the place where his house had been, all he could see was a pile of rocks and a piece of clothesline still strung with frozen laundry. Somewhere below that sad marker were his wife and children. Bill Warrington, tough coal miner, broke down and wept.

The rescue of the seventeen miners gave many people in Frank something to be thankful for as dusk brought a wretched day to a close. But there was nothing to ease the pain for young Lillian Clark, who had already lost her mother and all her siblings. Her last hope had been that her father would be among the men who'd been saved. He wasn't.

No one knows for certain just how many people died in the Frank Slide. Only twelve bodies were recovered. The official death toll was put at seventy-six, but it was quite likely higher; perhaps over 100. Nobody knew exactly how many men had been in the workers' camps. Because the area of destruction was so wide, and the cover of rock so deep, it was impossible to dig it all out in a search for human remains.

The Frank coal mine was eventually reopened, but its operation was short-lived. It closed for good in 1908. The people of Frank moved to a new community on the outskirts of Blairmore, Alberta. As the years passed, people forgot about the calamity that had swept Frank off the Canadian map. Today the scar on the side of Turtle Mountain is still visible, and at the Frank Slide Interpretation Centre visitors can learn all the details of the story. It is a story that Lillian Clark, Lester Johnston, and Marion Leitch would be reminded of for the rest of their lives, though they were only young-sters on that night the mountain walked.

6

· · · · · — — · · ·

THE TRIANGLE FIRE
"LET 'EM BURN"

The Triangle Shirtwaist Factory was typical of the thousands of "sweatshops" that were the shame of industrial America in the early twentieth century. It occupied the top three floors of the ten-story Asch Building at the corner of Green Street and Washington Place, near New York City's Washington Square and was owned by tycoons Max Blanck and Isaac Harris. Like many owners of these workhouses, they were unscrupulous in their desire to keep costs low and profits high. They exploited their employees ruthlessly, and paid little heed to safety in the workplace. In 1909 the Triangle workers had gone on strike for safer working conditions and better pay. But Blanck and Harris, like most company owners, detested workers' unions. With government and police on their side, they soon broke the strike.

Most of the interior of the Asch Building was made of wood. Passageways were narrow and poorly lit. Only one stairway went all the way up to the roof. Doors opened inwards that should have opened outwards. They were locked when they should have been unlocked. The building had no sprinkler system. There was but one fire escape, a narrow, iron ladder at the back of the building. It went down only to the second floor, and many employees, most of whom were immigrant workers, did not even know it was there. They had never had a fire drill. The attitude of the bosses toward immigrant workers was illustrated by one employer when a city official suggested he hold fire drills. "Let 'em burn," the man responded. "They're cattle anyway!"

~~~

Rose Glantz was in the women's dressing room, singing a popular song, "Every Little Movement Has a Meaning All Its Own." The young woman had good reason to be cheerful. It was 4:45 on a Saturday afternoon; quitting time at the end of her six-day work week. She would have a whole day off before the fifty-two-hour weekly grind began again early Monday morning. Several of her friends joined her in that dressing room on the ninth floor of the Asch Building, and soon they were all giggling. Rose and her companions didn't know that just below them on the eighth floor, fellow workers were already fleeing for their lives. They didn't know that within the next twenty minutes, 146 people would be dead or dying. It was March 25, 1911, and the Triangle Shirtwaist Factory was about to become the site of one of the deadliest fires in New York City's history.

About 500 people — most of them women and girls, some as young as 14 — toiled long, monotonous hours at Triangle making shirtwaists, a type of blouse very popular with women at that time. The majority of the workers were from immigrant families. Some spoke little or no English. They worked in dangerous, unsanitary conditions for as little as three dollars a week. The bosses would even adjust the time clocks to squeeze some extra "free" work out of their people. Yet, the immigrant poor would be so desperate for jobs, that they would pay bribes to supervisors or foremen to get family members jobs in the factory.

When female employees finished their shift, they had to line up at the exit and submit to having their purses searched before they could go home. Most of them could not afford to buy the fashionable shirtwaists they had been making all day, and the owners wanted to be sure that nobody stole them. Evidence would later show that theft in the Triangle factory was almost non-existent.

Up in the cutting room on the eighth floor, Eva Harris, sister of co-owner Isaac, smelled smoke and called to production manager Samuel Bernstein, "There is a fire, Mr. Bernstein!"

Bernstein saw flames and smoke, probably in a bin of rags on the Green Street side of the room. Eva ran to the exit and down the stairway. Some men threw pails of water on the fire, but the flames were already racing through

The blackened shell of the ninth floor New York's Asch Building had been a busy place where dozens of young women sewed blouses under sweatshop conditions. Many jumped from the windows to their deaths rather than being burned alive.

the workshop. Sparks landed on piles of tinder-dry cotton fabric, setting them ablaze. In no time the flames were licking at the wooden fixtures and work tables. Bernstein ran for the fire hose in the stairwell. He aimed the nozzle at the fire. No water came out.

Women and girls ran screaming for the exit, through which they could only pass one at a time. The stairway was partially blocked by Eva Harris, who had fainted before she could reach the seventh-floor landing. Panic-stricken women stumbled over her in their mad rush to get out. Eva was finally roused and helped to her feet by a police officer who had dashed into the building after seeing windows pop out because of the intense heat.

With the fire clearly out of control, Bernstein tried to evacuate the room. Some girls wanted to grab their clothes from the dressing room, but he stopped them. "One of the girls I slapped across the face because she was fainting," he reported later. "I got her out. I drove them out."

Newspapers of the day ran stories and cartoons about the bad conditions of the factory, but the owners were acquitted of manslaughter charges.

A machinist named Louis Brown opened a window next to the fire escape. Several women and girls went out and climbed down to the sixth floor. Someone managed to pry open the shutters on the window there, and the terrified women climbed in. Then they found that they were trapped by a locked door. They pounded on it until a policeman on the other side heard them and broke the door down.

The flames quickly spread up to the ninth floor, where sewing machine operators stitched the shirtwaists together. Then the fire reached the tenth floor, where the executive offices were located. Most of the people there were able to escape to the roof. But the ninth floor was a death trap for many. Escape routes were barred by locked doors. Even where doors were not locked, the press of dozens of terrified people against them made them impossible to pull open.

Rose Glantz and her friends came out of the dressing room into a scene from hell. There was fire all around and flames were coming in through windows. Rose was lucky. She was able to escape down the Green Street stairs. She had to run through flames at the eighth floor level and got burned when her scarf caught fire, but she made it to the ground. For others, that route quickly became impassable.

The two young men who operated the passenger elevators, Gaspar Mortillalo and Joseph Zito, risked their lives trying to take as many people down as they could. They made seven or eight trips up through smoke and flames in their rickety little cages. Each time they opened the gates, frightened workers fought to get in. The elevators were designed to hold only fifteen people each, but Zito recalled later that he was cramming them with twice that number. Katie Weiner was the last person to get into an elevator on its last trip from the ninth floor. She jumped in, and was lying on the heads of people packed in so tightly they couldn't move their arms.

As the elevator descended, the people in it heard loud thumps above them – the sickening sound of people falling down the shaft and landing on top of the elevator cage. The shaft became jammed with bodies. There would be no more elevator rescues.

Dozens of people climbed out the window to the spindly fire escape. In their crazed rush to get down, they pushed and climbed over each other. The ones who reached the bottom, still a story from the ground, were shoved off by those above them. They fell into a concrete courtyard.

The weight of all those clambering people was too much, and the bolts securing the iron ladder to the wall gave way. The fire escape tipped away from the building, plunging the shrieking women to their deaths.

Now each person trapped on the ninth floor faced a terrible decision. Stay and be roasted alive, or jump out a window to a quick death on the pavement below. The choice made by many provided a horrific spectacle that onlookers in the street would remember for the rest of their lives.

The New York City Fire Department had arrived within minutes of the alarm, but the firefighters' ladders could reach no higher than the sixth floor. Nor could the streams of water from their hoses reach high enough to benefit those who were trapped. The firemen would have to fight their way up through the building. But that would take precious minutes that the poor souls on the ninth floor didn't have.

As the growing crowd in the street watched, something that looked like a bale of cloth came out of a window. But it wasn't a bale of cloth. It was a girl. The body slammed into the ground with a horrifying thud, and the first jumper was dead. More came down, to be followed by still more. Some were on fire, blazing like comets. One girl stood on the ledge, tossed away her hat, poured out the contents of her purse, and then leapt into eternity just as her coins hit the pavement with a loud ring.

Pairs of girls embraced, and then plummeted to their deaths together. While some of the jumpers went feet first, with their arms outspread as though they could fly, others fell forward and plunged down headfirst. One girl made a desperate attempt to jump onto a fire ladder, three stories below her. She missed.

A newspaper reporter named Sam Sheppard witnessed the mass suicide and wrote a moving account of what he called "a love affair in the midst of all the horror." He watched a young man help three girls make the jump. "He saw that a terrible death awaited them in the flames," Sheppard wrote, "and his was only a terrible chivalry. He brought another girl to the window. I saw her put her arms around him and kiss him. Then he held her into space and dropped her. Quick as a flash, he was on the windowsill himself. His coat fluttered upwards, the air filled his trouser legs as he came down. We found later that in the room in which he stood, many girls were burning to death. He chose the easiest way and was brave enough to help the girl he loved to an easier death."

People in the street screamed, "Don't jump! Don't jump!" to the victims on the ledge and in the windows. But anything was better than death by fire. The firemen and some volunteers tried to catch the falling bodies in blankets, tarpaulins, and safety nets. But there were too many, coming too fast. Those who did hit the nets and tarps fell with such velocity that they ripped right through them or tore them from the men's hands. One girl was caught by a safety net, but the impact of her landing was too great. She climbed out of the net, walked a few steps, and fell dead.

The scene on the street was bedlam. Police tried to hold back the steadily growing crowd. Fire horses, terrified by the smell of blood, screamed and kicked in their harnesses. Flaming bodies continued to drop. Triangle employees who had escaped to the ground floor were prevented from leaving the building by firemen, so they wouldn't be struck by falling bodies. Then a solitary figure in burning clothes fell from the ninth floor. It caught on a hook protruding from a ledge at the sixth floor and hung there for a moment, then dropped to the sidewalk. That was the last body to fall. The time was 4:57: only twelve minutes since the fire had started.

The people who had made it to the roof – most of them from the tenth floor executive offices – were taken off by means of ladders extended from the next building. Among them were owner Max Blanck and his daughters, Henrietta, 12, and Mildred, 5. They had been about to go shopping with their father when the fire broke out. They owed their lives to Samuel Bernstein, who had come up from the eighth floor and taken charge when Blanck had apparently been paralyzed by shock and indecision.

Blanck's partner, Isaac Harris, had also made it to the roof, gallantly leading a group of girls with scorched clothing and smoldering hair. But Harris' show of leadership in the moments of danger would be heavily outbalanced by the barrage of accusations to come. The tragedy, after all, need never have happened.

For some of the survivors the brush with death had been very close indeed. Sixteen-year-old Abe Gordon had been in the frenzied climb down the fire escape. He sensed that it was not going to hold. When Abe reached the sixth floor window, he started to climb inside.

"I stepped back into the building," he said later. "I still had a foot on the fire escape when I heard a loud noise and looked back up. The people were falling all around me, screaming all around me. The fire escape was collapsing."

Ethel Monick, 16, was at a window and ready to jump. "Then I saw in my mind how I would look, lying there on the sidewalk and I got ashamed. I moved back from the window." Ethel was one of the lucky girls who got down in an elevator.

Cecelia Walker had been in the crush of people at an elevator doorway. The elevator was on its way down. Suddenly Cecelia found herself at the very edge of the threshold, being pushed into the shaft. She tried to hang on, but she knew that at any moment she was going to fall. With one hand in a muff, she leapt forward and grabbed the elevator cable. She would remember sliding down as far as the fifth floor. Then something hit her. Cecelia was found at the bottom of a pile of bodies on top of the elevator. She awoke in hospital with head injuries, a broken arm and a broken finger.

Once firemen got into the building, it took them only minutes to extinguish the fire. But everywhere there was cruel evidence of the difference a few minutes can make. There were charred bodies in the elevator shafts, dead piled up behind locked doors, and corpses amidst the remains of sewing machines on the ninth floor. More bodies lay in the courtyard at the back. And there were all those broken human shells out on the street.

Among the dead were Laura Brunette, 17, Tina Frank, 17, Samuel Tabick, 18, and Ida Brodsky, 16. A few, *very* few, were found with a spark of life still flickering and were rushed to hospital, where they subsequently died. These included Ida Kenowitz, 18, Sarah Kupla, 16, Becky Nebrerer, 19, and Anna Nicholas, 18. Of the 146 people who died, sixty-three were teenagers. Of those, all but five were girls.

The bodies were taken to an enclosed pier that was converted into a temporary morgue. There they were laid out in coffins while crowds of grief stricken relatives and friends who were missing loved ones awaited admission, hoping against hope that the ones they sought would not be there.

For many, gut-wrenching fear became numb reality when they looked into a numbered coffin. Morris Altman found his sister Annie, 16. Meyer Sabasowitz found his daughter Sarah, 17. Rosie Sorkin, 18, was identified by her uncle, Louis Sorkin. Serafino Maltese found not only his wife, Catherine, but also his daughters Lucia, 20, and little 14-year-old Rosaria.

Many of the dead had been burned or pulverized beyond recognition and had to be identified by possessions or some other means. Jacob Goldstein knew his sister by the buttons on her shoes. Dominic Leone identified his niece by a lock of her hair. Esther Rosen knew she had found her brother when she saw his signet ring. All were teenagers.

Not all of the hordes of people who swarmed down to "Misery Row," as the pier came to be called, had a legitimate reason for being there. Thousands were just morbidly curious. Pickpockets posing as friends and relatives of the deceased tried to bluff their way past the police. Their ghoulish intent was to rob the dead of jewelry and other "souvenirs" that could be sold in the street.

The public was outraged over the loss of life in the Triangle disaster. There were five official inquiries. Blanck and Harris were tried for manslaughter, but were acquitted. Mr. Asch, when questioned about the safety of his building, replied, "I never gave the matter a thought."

When Asch argued that his building met the fire-safety requirements of the time, in many respects he was technically correct. Wealthy men such as he had used their influence to ensure that laws would not interfere with their profits. Workers' unions would eventually become strong enough to pressure governments into passing legislation to improve safety in the workplace. In the United States, Canada, and other industrialized nations, sweatshops like the Triangle factory became things of the past. Unfortunately, they have not disappeared from the face of the earth. In the developing nations of Latin America, Africa, and Asia, clothing, toys, and a shopper's catalogue full of other items are manufactured by underpaid workers, including children, in sweatshop conditions. These commodities can be found on store shelves all over North America and the rest of the Western World. The Triangle factories of the early twentieth century have merely changed locations.

7

· · · — — · · ·

THE HALIFAX EXPLOSION
"THE SKY OPENED."

Early in the morning of December 6, 1917, the French ship Mont Blanc sailed into the port of Halifax, Nova Scotia. The vessel had come from New York, packed with munitions destined for the World War I battlefields of Europe. The Mont Blanc's captain hoped to join a convoy for the Atlantic crossing, for protection from German submarines. He should have been flying a red flag to warn people of his deadly cargo, but was not. Through a series of navigational errors that are still disputed today, the Mont Blanc collided with a Norwegian relief ship, the Imo. The Mont Blanc caught fire, and the captain and crew immediately abandoned ship and raced for safety in a lifeboat. The burning vessel, loaded with more than 2,500 tons of explosives drifted toward the Halifax docks and the city's North End district, called Richmond, a community of factories, schools, and working class families. The stage was set for the biggest man-made, nonnuclear explosion in history, and one of the worst disasters ever to befall a North American city.

~~

Looking out of a cloakroom window in St. Joseph's Roman Catholic School, 11-year-old Cecelia McGrath saw a pillar of smoke and flames rising from a ship in Halifax Harbour. Like thousands of other Haligonians that morning, Cecelia was fascinated by the spectacle. A ship afire in the stretch of water called The Narrows in the well-protected Port of Halifax was a rare sight indeed. All along the Halifax shore and the waterfront of the smaller town of

Dartmouth on the opposite side of the Narrows, people were watching the dramatic show on the water.

In the Orr household in Richmond, Annie Orr and her six children watched from a window of their brand new home. Barbara, 14, her sister Isabel, 6, and brother Ian, 11, left the house to go down to the docks for a closer look. Barbara took a detour through Mulgrave Park so she could call on a friend, but Ian and Isabel made a beeline straight for the waterfront. Not far away, on Gottingen Street, Barbara's cousin Gladys Orr, 11, watched the burning ship from the front yard of her home with her mother and 5-year-old brother Bill.

Elsie Bauer, 14, was on her way to the Bloomfield School when she met a friend. The other girl said, "Come, Elsie, let's go down and see the ship burning in the harbor." But Elsie replied, "No, I don't want to be late for school." Elsie continued on her way, while her friend hurried off to join scores of other children who, on the last morning of their lives, were diverted from the routine path between home and school by the conflagration in Halifax Harbour. No one knew that the burning ship was a floating bomb.

At four minutes past 9:00, Cecelia McGrath decided that she had better tell one of the nuns who taught at St. Joseph's about the fire down on the water She turned away from the window. That split-second movement undoubtedly saved her eyes – and quite likely her life.

At that precise moment, the lives of ordinary people, doing ordinary things, were about to change forever. In Bloomfield School, Roland Theakston, 14, was escorting a line of thirty-five small boys up a stairway to the Assembly Hall. On East Young Street, 8-year-old Norman Roberts was sitting in the kitchen of his family's apartment with his mother and sister Mabel, aged 2. In Elsie Bauer's house, her little sister Jean had just opened the door of a birdcage to play with her pet canary. In a school called the County Academy, assembled students were singing a hymn, "Peace, Perfect Peace." Nine-year-old Pearl Hartlen, who hadn't gone to school that day, was home with her mother. Agnes Foran, 12, had not gone to school either. She and her mother were standing at a window of their home on Merkel Street, watching the *Mont Blanc* burn. Suddenly, as Agnes would put it later, "The sky opened."

Fascinated residents watched as a tugboat skipper brought his vessel alongside the *Mont Blanc* to try to fight the blaze with his firehose. Sailors from Canadian and British naval vessels had gone out in small boats and were just boarding the *Mont Blanc*. Their plan may have been to steer the ship away from the city and sink her in deep water. Whatever their intentions, those courageous men never had a chance to carry them out.

The blast that disintegrated the *Mont Blanc* and the men climbing up her sides shot smoke and flames five miles (8 km) into the sky. The boom was heard as far away as Prince Edward Island and it caused an earthquake that was felt in Sydney, Cape Breton, 270 miles (435 km) away. The explosion blew the water out of Halifax Harbour, sending a massive tidal wave smashing ashore. Buildings that weren't crushed by the tsunami were flattened by the concussion that followed. A rain of molten metal and rocks from the sea floor poured down upon Halifax. The *Mont Blanc's* anchor and one of the ship's big guns landed in locations 3 miles (4.8 km) from ground zero, but 6 miles (9.6 km) apart.

As a huge mushroom cloud billowed above the smashed city, fires caused by molten steel and overturned coal stoves broke out everywhere. People who had not been killed by the explosion but were trapped in wrecked buildings were roasted alive. The blast had instantly decimated the Halifax Fire Department.

The destruction within Halifax Harbour itself was frightful. Ships were capsized or blown right out of the water. The relief ship *Imo* was tossed onto the Dartmouth shore like a child's toy boat. Scores of merchant sailors and naval men were killed or injured.

But it was in the city's North End that the carnage was worst. Two square miles (5 sq. km) of Atlantic Canada's biggest city had been erased. Even in areas of Halifax farthest from the blast, scarcely a window remained intact. Aside from the explosion itself, flying glass would be the principal cause of death and injury. Dagger-like shards of glass shot across rooms and sliced into faces and bodies. Many survivors were partially or totally blinded for life. A nurse would later report seeing a bucketful of eyeballs in an emergency ward.

As Cecelia McGrath turned away from the cloakroom window, a thunder-clap unlike anything she had ever heard filled the air. The school swayed violently. Glass from the window she'd had her face pressed against just seconds earlier slashed past her. Amazingly, she was not cut.

Cecelia did not panic. She looked into her classroom and saw that part of the floor had collapsed, dropping children into the room below. Carefully making her way across the gaping space on floor supports that were still intact, Cecelia reached a window. She climbed over the sill and lowered herself until she was hanging by her hands. Then she dropped a story-and-a-half to the ground, unhurt. Eight other girls followed her example and successfully escaped from the shattered school.

Throughout the rubble of St. Joseph's school the nuns, some of them blinded by blood running into their eyes, struggled to pull children out of the debris and take them to safety. One Sister cried, "My heavenly God! The Germans have arrived!" Many people did in fact think that the city was under attack from German warships or zeppelins.

Three little girls lay crushed to death in the school. Fifteen more lay dead in the schoolyard, scattered like so many leaves. Cecelia McGrath ran home through a landscape of horror. Bodies and pieces of bodies lay everywhere. Wounded people, bloody and blackened by smoke, staggered around in shock. Some were naked, and seemed entirely unaware of it. When Cecelia reached what had once been her street, she found her house in flames, with her mother inside.

In Mulgrave Park the blast of air snatched up Barbara Orr and threw her a quarter of a mile. When the teenager hit the ground she shattered one leg. Barbara tried to crawl toward home, but smoke and fire barred the way. She turned instead in the direction of her uncle's house on Gottingen Street. Like Cecelia, Barbara passed through a nightmare of broken bodies and screaming wounded. When she finally reached her destination, her Aunt Edna and cousin Gladys didn't recognize her at first. She was black from head to toe with soot and oil. Barbara didn't know it yet, but her mother, father, and all of her brothers and sisters were dead.

The two buildings of the Bloomfield School were wrecked. The explosion shattered windows, tore off roofs, and shook the walls. Pupils and teachers were buried in plaster and debris. Roland Theakston, who had been leading the little boys under his supervision up a flight of stairs, told them to make an about face. He took them back down, and outside. Thanks to his cool-headedness and the fire drills the children had practiced, all of the boys exited the building safely. For many of those children, however, there would be no home and no family to which they could return.

Elsie Bauer had arrived at school and was climbing a staircase when the blast ripped through the morning air. One moment she was about to set foot on the third floor landing; the next thing she knew, she was sitting under a tree in the schoolyard. She was dazed, her face bloody and her hair full of glass splinters. Her schoolmates were on the ground all around her. Elsie was the only one moving. In the hours to come she would learn that her sister and brother were dead, and that her mother had lost an eye. She never again saw the friend who had played hooky to watch the burning ship.

The students of the County Academy had the last notes of "Peace, Perfect Peace" blasted away by an ear-splitting roar and the crash of shattering glass. Here, too, the fire-drill discipline the children had learned prevailed over panic. They left the building in good order. Most of them had been cut or bruised, but the injuries were minor.

That school had been relatively lucky. Not so the Richmond Public School and the Protestant Orphanage. One hundred children had their lives snuffed out in the Richmond School, and twenty-seven more perished in the Orphanage. Rescue workers would weep openly as they pulled the small, mangled bodies out of the rubble.

There were many acts of heroism in Halifax that terrible day. Soldiers and navy men risked their lives to prevent the fires from reaching military stores of explosives and ammunition. Civilians who could still function clawed through the wreckage to rescue wounded victims. Some of those who became heroes that day were children.

The explosion sent furniture flying in Norman Roberts' home, and set it on fire. Norman and his little sister Mabel were not badly hurt, but their mother was unconscious on the floor, under a pile of furniture. At first Norman threw burning objects out the window, thinking he could stop the fire from spreading. When he realized that it was no use, he carried his sister outside. Then he went back into the building and dragged his mother out just before flames engulfed the place. When Mrs. Roberts came to, she was several blocks away from her burning home.

The blast flattened the Hartlen home. Pearl pulled herself free of the wreckage, then found her mother buried under the ruins. She had been knocked out by a blow to the head. Pearl started to drag her mother out, but Mrs. Hartlen's skirt was snagged on something. Lacking anything with which to cut the material, Pearl bit and tore at the fabric with her teeth until she was able to free her mother and drag her to safety.

Agnes Foran showed remarkable bravery for an adolescent. She and her mother were both thrown to the floor when their windows were blown in. The house did not collapse on them, but Mrs. Foran had been blinded by flying glass. Agnes quickly got some water and pieces of cloth and bathed her mother's eyes. Then she led her out to the street and went back into the house for her baby brother, whom she found safe in his carriage.

Agnes left her mother and the baby, and ran up and down ruined streets in search of help. She could find no one who was able to assist her, and so she returned to her wounded mother. All she could do was sit there amidst the chaos and hope that someone would come to their aid.

At about 10:30 Agnes' father, who had been at work when the disaster struck, managed to make his way to what was left of his home. When he found his wife and children, Agnes was on the verge of passing out. Mr. Foran found a chair for her, and examined her body. The girl was covered with cuts, and her clothes were saturated with blood. Mr. Foran somehow got hold of a man with a car, and took his family to Victoria Hospital, which was already overflowing with blast victims. It was several hours before a doctor could look at Agnes. What he found was incredible.

A piece of glass half the size of an adult's hand had been driven into Agnes' stomach, and only a tiny point was visible above the skin. The doctor operated to remove the glass. It took twenty-nine stitches to close the wound in the child's abdomen. Happily, Agnes recovered fully.

All through the smoking devastation of the North End, soldiers, police, and Boy Scouts tore through wreckage in search of survivors. Some babies and small children were passed through several hands before they finally reached a hospital or aid station. This would lead to some confusion and heartbreak for families trying to locate missing children.

One of the most amazing stories of survival and mistaken identity involved Private Benjamin Henneberry, who had just returned home from the war in France. The explosion destroyed the apartment building in which his family lived. Private Henneberry survived the blast, but could find no sign of his wife and five children. He heard a moan come from a pile of debris, and began to dig through it with his bare hands. A group of soldiers assisted him. The men uncovered an iron coal stove with its ash pan pulled out. Beneath the ash pan was a squalling baby girl. The child was slightly burned, but the ash pan had protected her from being crushed. Henneberry was certain that she was his 8-month-old daughter Olive. At Pine Hill Hospital, however, the baby was identified as 18-month-old Annie Liggins.

News of the little girl's miraculous survival spread quickly. The newspapers dubbed her "Ashpan Annie." Sadly for Private Henneberry, his wife and children were all found dead.

Ill fortune was not finished with the people of Halifax. That night a major blizzard howled down on a city in which there was hardly a window with glass to keep out the

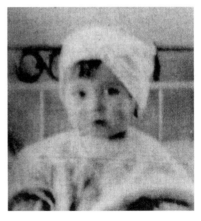

Little Annie Liggins was dug out from under an iron coal stove. Annie was found screaming under the ash pan and was dubbed Ashpan Annie. She was protected by the pan and had only minor burns.

The 1917 explosion in Halifax Harbour was so intense that windows all over the city blew out, causing horrific damage to the eyes of those who had been looking out windows at the ships on fire in the bay. Nurses reported seeing buckets of eyeballs in hospital wards as the survivors were being treated.

snow and the cold. Thousands of people whose homes had been destroyed were sheltered in tents that the army set up in parks, but they had no heat. The storm hampered rescue operations, and many injured victims who might have been saved froze to death.

The Halifax Explosion destroyed more than 1,600 buildings. Many more were damaged beyond repair. More than 1,600 people were killed by the blast. Hundreds more would die from their injuries, bringing the number of dead to almost 2,000. The list of dead and missing included 586 children and teenagers. Of the more than 9,000 who were injured, many lost limbs or the use of their eyes, or were permanently disfigured. Almost 10,000 were homeless.

When news of the disaster reached the outside world, relief began to flow into Halifax from across Canada and the United States, and from Great Britain, Australia, and New Zealand. Americans in the New England states, with whom Nova Scotians had always had close ties, were especially generous. Doctors and nurses from cities like Boston and Providence headed north on trains loaded with medical supplies. To commemorate this act of compassion, every year the city of Halifax sends the city of Boston the gift of a huge Christmas tree.

As the people of Halifax buried their dead and began to clean up and rebuild their city, there was much debate over who was responsible for the calamity. An official inquiry would point the finger of blame at the captains of both the Imo *and the* Mont Blanc. *It was recommended that regulations dealing with the transport of munitions through Halifax Harbour be reviewed. But when all was said and done, the real villain on that terrible December day was the war. In an interview she gave many years later, Helen Loomer Sweet, who was a child at the time of the explosion, recalled her first reaction to the disaster: "I thought, if this is war, I wouldn't want any part of it."*

8

· · · · — — · · ·

THE LAURIER PALACE FIRE
DEADLY PANIC

January 9, 1927, was to have been a special day for René Roy of Montreal. It was his 14th birthday, and as a treat he and his brother were being allowed to go to the matinee at the Laurier Palace Theatre, a movie house on Ste. Catherine Street. The old Palace was very popular with Montreal children and adolescents because its owner, Ameen Lawand, ignored the Quebec provincial law that said children under the age of 16 could not be admitted to a movie house unless accompanied by an adult. At the Palace, any kid who had the fifteen cents admission price was allowed in. Lawand was also in violation of a long list of other regulations. The two stairways to the balcony were narrow and dark, with sharp turns and no railings. The highly flammable reels of film were improperly stored. The seats in the lower auditorium and on the balcony exceeded the number permitted by law. Lawand further overcrowded the place by allowing children who could not find seats to stand in the aisles. He did not even keep fire exits clear. The ushers on his staff, some of whom weren't much more than boys, had no training in emergency procedures. Lawand had been fined several times for these and other infractions. That very morning a constable had reprimanded him because of a blocked fire exit. The Laurier Palace should, in fact, have been closed down. But it was said, though never proven, that Lawand had connections at City Hall.

~~~

About 800 children and teenagers made their way to the Palace that bright winter day in 1927. Among them were Philip Martel, 12, who had his sisters

Eva, 8, and Yvette, 7, in tow. Thirteen-year-old Adrien Quintal had his younger siblings Hildegarde and Sylvia with him. It was Sylvia's very first visit to a movie house. Loretta Francoeur, 14, was another who was excited at the prospect of seeing "moving pictures" for the first time. Though the popularity of movies had been growing for over two decades, some parents were slow to acknowledge them as an acceptable form of entertainment for children. The Bishop of Montreal, a powerful force in Catholic Quebec, took a dim view of them and did not think that movie houses should even be permitted to open on Sundays, much less admit minors.

Joining the parade of young moviegoers were 16-year-old Antoine Girourd and 8-year-old Gaston Arpin, son of a Montreal fireman. Roger Frappier, 13, went with his half-brothers Roland and Paul Leduc, aged 11 and 12. Ernie Fitzpatrick, 14, was accompanied by his pals the Murphy brothers, Michael, 11, and Eddie, 12.

The Martel and Quintal children, and Loretta Francoeur, were among the few who had their parents' permission to be at the Palace that day. Later investigation would reveal that 75 percent of the children at the Palace that afternoon were there without their parents' knowledge or consent. Montreal police officer Albert Boisseau thought that his children Germaine, 13, Roland, 11, and Yvette, 8, had gone skating. Adrien Metu, 10, had his father's permission to go to the movies, but *not* to the Laurier Palace. That place, Joseph Metu argued, was not safe. He had been in there, and he didn't think it had enough exits.

Owner Ameen Lawand was not at the Palace when the children began to line up out front at about noon. He had gone to the Maisonneuve, his other movie house, and had left the Palace in the charge of assistant manager Michel Arle. Aside from a handful of adults who had taken their children to the movies, Arle, head usher Camil Bazzy, projectionist Emile Massicote, and the woman in the ticket booth were the only adults in the Palace that day.

There was much laughter and jostling as the children plunked down their nickels and dimes and filed inside. In the front windows and on the walls of the lobby, posters advertised the films that were playing: *Upstage,* a drama; *The Devil's Gulch,* a western; and the comedy that the children were all anxious to see, *Get 'em Young.* There would be something grimly ironic about that last title. Other posters advertised the coming week's attraction, *Sparrows,* starring Canadian-born movie queen Mary Pickford.

Once the children had bought their candy, they dashed for the best seats. Those who were farther back in the lineup would have to stand in the aisles. By the time Ernie Fitzpatrick and the Murphy brothers got in, the lower auditorium was full and they had to go upstairs to the balcony. Michael quickly claimed the last empty seat. Ernie and Eddie – and dozens of other children – had to stand. There were about 500 people, mostly teenagers, in the lower auditorium. The majority of the nearly 350 jammed into the balcony were younger children.

The opening film began at 12:30. As the black-and-white images flickered on the big screen, the children cheered the heroes and booed the villains. They munched candy and shrugged off their coats as the theater became too warm. Movies were still silent at that time, and the older children read the written dialogue for the little ones. Overhead, cigarette smoke curled in the beam of light from the projection room.

For about ninety minutes the Palace was filled with the noisy pandemonium of a movie house packed with unchaperoned children. Then, shortly after two o'clock, as the young audience laughed at the slapstick antics of the characters in *Get 'em Young,* someone yelled "Fire! Fire!" Shrieks of laughter quickly became screams of terror.

At the cry of "Fire!" the people in the lower auditorium immediately left their seats and exited through the front and back doors. That part of the Palace was cleared without a hitch or a casualty. But up on the balcony, fear and confusion quickly became panic.

With one exception, the ushers did not know what to do. One or two tried throwing water on the fire, but the blaze was already beyond this feeble attempt to control it. Some ushers told the children to run, while others told them to remain seated. As the smoke thickened and the flames began to lick at the wooden seats, the mob of frightened children surged toward the two stairways.

At the west stairway an usher named Paul Champagne took charge. He told the children not to try to go through the door all at once. Under his direction they filed through one at a time. Champagne escorted them down to the lobby and out to the street. Then he tried to go back up to the balcony, but smoke forced him to retreat.

On the east stairway, though, all was bedlam. The first children to run down turned a corner and were confronted by assistant manager Arle. He stood at the bottom of the stairs and told them to return to their seats. Eighteen-year-old Romeo Colin was there.

"I had almost got downstairs when this man held out his arms and told us to go back again. When the man stopped us, we obeyed, for we thought it might have been a little joke. So we went up again. There was a mass of children rushing out. A girl had fainted and I picked her up and carried her downstairs on my back. I don't know what happened then, for I was pulled out myself." The Montreal Chief of Police would later commend Romeo for saving the girl.

The children going back up the stairs met the rush of other children trying to get out. They turned and fled pell-mell back down. By this time Arle had run out to the street. Head usher Bazzy was nowhere to be seen. A few of the children on the east stairway did manage to escape. Paul Leduc somehow crawled on his belly through the crush on the stairs and reached the lobby. Ernie Fitzpatrick reached safety by climbing over people's heads.

Then, as the children struggled desperately to jam past each other in the narrow stairwell, someone fell, blocking the passageway. One child after another, pushed from behind, fell onto the heap. Somehow the door at the foot of the stairs was pushed closed. Because it opened inward, it was jammed shut by the growing pile of bodies behind it.

Up on the balcony where the air was now thick with smoke, children pushed, shoved, and dragged each other aside as they fought to get through the doorway. Philip Martel tried to hold onto Eva and Yvette, but was dragged away from them. René Roy and his brother became separated.

Roger Frappier lost the Leduc brothers in the confusion. Roger was one of the few who kept his head. He was choking on smoke and realized that he had no chance of escaping down the stairs. He went to the edge of the balcony, climbed over the rail and jumped. He was slightly injured when he landed in an aisle, but as he said later, "I was too excited to notice it." Roger limped out the front door to the safety of the street.

When projectionist Emile Massicote realized what was happening, he did not think first of his own safety as Arle and Bazzy had done. His projection room had a window that overlooked the Palace's marquee. Massicote hurried out to the mob of children struggling at the doorway and shouted to them to go out through the projection room. The shrieking, crying children didn't even hear him.

Massicote grabbed two hysterical children and dragged them, kicking and howling, into the projection room. He pushed them out the window onto the marquee. Then he went back for two more. Massicote rescued thirty children that way, until smoke forced him to climb out onto the marquee himself.

The east stairway was now a death trap. Once a child fell, he or she could not get back up as more bodies fell on top. They were soon packed eight deep, and thick smoke billowed down the stairway. Those who did not choke to death on the smoke were asphyxiated by the sheer weight of the bodies piled on top of them. In the words of one newspaper reporter, the stairway was, "a solid, suffocating, groaning, shrieking and dying mass."

Firemen and police were on the scene quickly. Officers moved back the crowd that was gathering in front of the Palace, while firemen put up ladders to take the children off the marquee. Others rushed inside. In the lobby they found the first victims. Two little girls, suffocated by smoke, lay dead beneath the poster for *Swallows*. A man, alive but unconscious, lay across the bodies of two more children.

One group of firemen ran up the west stairway to deal with the fire, which they easily extinguished. Another group tried to get into the east stairway but could not open the door. They chopped a hole through a washroom wall, and then saw the heart-rending scene in the stairway. Piled up against the door, wedged in the narrow space between the walls was a great tangle of small bodies. There was very little sign of movement and only an occasional groan or whimper. So tightly were the bodies packed, that it took several strong

An afternoon at the movies turned out to be the last day on earth for seventy-eight children crowded into the Laurier Palace in Montreal. This time the owner served jail time for overcrowding, allowing unaccompanied minors to attend, not keeping fire exits clear, and for having no emergency plans in effect.

firemen and constables pulling together to extract just one dead boy.

One by one the rescuers pulled the limp forms out through the hole until they could open the door. Some were alive, but injured. One of these was Antoine Girourd, who had slight burns and a concussion. From a hospital bed he later described his ordeal:

"I noticed flames shoot up through a crack in the floor and immediately everyone rushed from the balcony. I got safely down the stairway to within five steps of the bottom, when I was knocked down by the rush on the stairway and fell, with people piled over me. Three dead boys were beneath me when the police raised me, and above me five or six injured boys had to be removed before I could be reached."

One of the firemen on the scene was Alphego Arpin, father of Gaston. As he and his colleagues carried out dead and injured children, he was sick with worry because he knew that Gaston had gone to the Palace that day. Later that afternoon, fireman Arpin found his son in the morgue.

Constable Albert Boisseau was off-duty that day, but when he heard of the emergency he hurried to the Palace to help. Not until he saw the body of his daughter Germaine among the dead did he realize to his horror that his children had not gone skating, as they had told him. He made a frantic search of the hospitals before he found Roland and Yvette in the morgue.

While ambulances and taxicabs rushed injured children to hospitals, policemen and firemen, some of them choking back sobs, laid the dead in a long row on the sidewalk. Police allowed frantic parents through the cordon. The sight that awaited them was both terrible and pitiful. Little faces were blackened with smoke. Torn clothes hung from battered bodies. One little girl still clutched a candy bar in her lifeless hand. A priest gave the last rites to two little boys who gasped out their names and then died.

Eddie Murphy was one of the children Emile Massicote had dragged to the marquee. His brother Michael, the "lucky" one who'd got a seat, was dead. René Roy's brother got out alive, but René died on his birthday. Philip Martel was alive in a hospital, but his sisters Eva and Yvette were dead. Adrien Metu, whose father had forbidden him to go to the Palace, was dead. So were Loretta Francoeur, Roland Leduc, Marcel Girard and the three Quintal children. Seventeen of the children who were rushed to hospital died, bringing the total list of dead to a numbing seventy-eight.

It would never be satisfactorily concluded just what started the fire up on the balcony. Ushers would later be accused of smoking on duty. They would testify that children frequently sneaked cigarettes into the movie house, and lit matches to look under seats. In all likelihood a carelessly discarded cigarette or match ignited the rubbish under the seats, and the flames soon spread to the dry old wood of the balcony floor. When Ameen Lawand heard of the disaster at the Palace, he immediately left the Maisonneuve. He went straight home and phoned his lawyer. Lawand would eventually be convicted of manslaughter and sentenced to two years in prison. Camil Bazzy and Michel Arle would be sentenced to one year each. Dozens of bereaved parents brought lawsuits against Lawand, but none were successful. The Laurier Palace fire was the deadliest movie house blaze in Canadian history. However, most of the victims had not been killed by flames or smoke. They had been crushed in the narrow stairway in that mad, panic-driven stampede.

After the Laurier Palace tragedy, municipalities across Canada reviewed fire safety regulations for movie houses and other public places. They passed strict laws and promised rigid enforcement. In the province of Quebec the law forbidding minors under the age of 16 to attend movies without adult accompaniment was stringently enforced. It would remain in effect until 1961.

9

· · · · · — — · · ·

THE NEWFOUNDLAND
TSUNAMI
TERROR FROM THE SEA

*O*n November 18, 1929, an earthquake registering 7.2 on the Richter scale
shook the island of Newfoundland. It was felt in Nova Scotia and even as
far away as New York City. The quake's epicenter was at the bottom of the
Atlantic Ocean about 350 miles (560 km) south of Newfoundland's capital, St. John's.
The shockwave of such an undersea disturbance may be barely noticeable as it passes
through deep water. A ship on the surface might not detect it at all. But as the wave nears
land and the water becomes shallower, the energy builds up into one of nature's most awe-
some forces. A tsunami, once incorrectly called a tidal wave, is a giant wave or series of
waves resulting from an undersea quake. It strikes coastal areas almost without warning
and with devastating effects. On that November day, such a monster was racing at speeds
of up to 80 miles (128.7 km) an hour toward Newfoundland's Burin Peninsula.

The people of the Burin Peninsula didn't know what to make of the "Big
Thump" – a violent tremor in the earth that shook their frame houses and
rattled the dishes on tables and shelves. In one of the many communities scattered along the rocky shore, people thought there had been an explosion
somewhere. In another, residents wondered if the local electric power plant
had been the cause.

Up and down the peninsula people ran from their houses in fear and
confusion. Earthquakes were rare in the history of Newfoundland. On that

afternoon few knew what was happening, much less what to do. Then, as suddenly as it had started, the shaking and rumbling stopped. Looking out to the Atlantic Ocean, residents noted that the sea was as calm as could be. Most of them concluded that whatever the commotion had been, it was all over. They went back to their homes.

However, in the little community of Lord's Cove, a man named Prosper Walsh knew better. He had sailed in the Caribbean and the waters off North Africa, and had experienced earthquakes and tsunamis. Walsh was playing cards with friends when the tremor hit. He immediately told the other men to get their families inland because a tidal wave would come. Then he went through the village, banging on doors and spreading the alarm. Some people listened to him. Some didn't.

The Burin Peninsula curves like a comma from the south coast of Newfoundland, just west of the larger Avalon Peninsula. In 1929, when Newfoundland was not yet a Canadian province but a self-governing Dominion within the British Empire, the peninsula had a population of about 13,000. These hardy people who took their livelihood from the sea lived in tiny communities, often located at the heads of small bays. A telegraph line connected the people on Burin with St. John's, but roads linking the peninsula to the main part of the island were rudimentary. Almost all transportation was by water. A typical fishing community consisted of a cluster of houses, most of which had vegetable gardens. Some families also kept chickens, a cow, and other livestock. Each waterfront had a wharf, platforms where fish were processed, called stages, and flakes, platforms where fish were dried. There were also "stores," which were not places of business but buildings where food, fuel, and fishing equipment were kept.

Life in these communities was tough. But with hard work, and an element of luck, a fisherman could provide well for his family. In most households, mothers baked bread daily, preserved food, and made most of the family's clothes. Children learned to help with chores at an early age.

When the ground shook in the village of Point au Gaul, Caroline Hillier, 12, ran out of the house with her mother, Lydia, and little brother, Ben.

Outside, an elderly man named Joe Miller was on his knees with an ear pressed to the ground. A small crowd gathered around him. Joe remained in this peculiar position for a few minutes, then stood up and told the people to prepare for a tidal wave.

No one took him seriously. How could there be any danger with the sea as smooth as glass? Caroline's family certainly didn't pay much attention to such talk. They were preparing to celebrate her father's birthday. It was the first time since his childhood that Thomas Hillier had even wanted to have a birthday party. As it turned out, it would be an ominous day to get together with old friends.

In the village of Lawn, 6-year-old Anna Tarrant was in bed with a sore throat when the earthquake struck. Her mother, Hilda, was just coming up from the root cellar with some vegetables, which she dropped as the house shook. Anna's father, Pat, rushed into the house and told Hilda to dress the children in warm clothes and take them to high ground. Pat had served in the Royal Navy and had witnessed an earthquake in the Indian Ocean. While the eldest son, Isadore, helped his mother with the younger children, Pat ran through the village pounding on doors and shouting at people to run up the hill that rose above their community. Pat Tarrant was a well-respected man in Lawn. With the exception of one elderly couple, everybody responded to his warning.

In her home in Kelly's Cove on Great Burin Island, Pearl Brushett, age 5, got ready for bed after the excitement over the tremor died down. She had to share the bed with her sisters Lottie, 8, and Lillian, 7. Pearl didn't mind, because on these cold autumn nights the girls kept each other warm. On this night, Lillian was suffering from an earache. Her mother, Carrie, had given her a heated plate wrapped in a blanket on which to lay her head. After tucking in the girls' brothers, 10-year-old Fred and baby James, Carrie went into the girls' room to kiss them goodnight. The children's father, William, was away getting the family's winter supply of firewood.

In another Kelly's Cove household, Frances Kelly and her daughter Dorothy were busy making pillowcases on the sewing machine when the tremor struck. Dorothy's older sister Marion, 13, had been visiting the nearby home of an elderly friend, but rushed home after the tremor. Once everyone had calmed down, the children had their supper and Marion and Frances curled Dorothy's hair. Young Curtis went out to play at the top of a nearby hill. His brother, Elroy, played in the yard. Their father, Vincent, had also gone away to the bush for firewood.

Sarah Rennie of Lord's Cove was busy with her sewing machine, too. She was so engaged in her work that she didn't even notice the tremor. Her youngest child, Bernard, 18 months, was in his high chair, tied in as a safety measure, a common practice in those days. Rita, 9, Patrick, 7, and Margaret, 4, played in the house. Sarah's husband Patrick was playing cards with Prosper Walsh. Their son Martin, 13, and his younger brother Albert had gone with their father.

In little Port Au Bras, a village that dated back to the 1700s, fisherman Tom Fudge and his sons John, 20, and Job, 13, were working in the family store when they felt the ground tremble. Tom's wife, Jessie, and their daughters Gertie, 15, Harriet, 11, and Hannah, 9, hurried down to the store. They were clearly frightened. Tom assured everyone that the earthquake wouldn't last long and that they had nothing to worry about. When the shaking stopped, Jessie took the girls back into the house. Tom, John, and Job continued with their work in the store.

And so it went in places like Lamaline, Allan's Island, and Taylor's Bay. Some residents took to the high ground and cast fearful glances at the seemingly tranquil ocean. Others decided that the tremor had been a curious but non-threatening phenomenon, and returned to their usual routines. For some that decision would prove fatal.

Just after 7:00 PM, about two hours after the tremor, the tsunami smashed into the Burin Peninsula. First the seawater was sucked away from the coast, leaving the seabed bare off little fishing ports along a 30-mile (48-km) stretch of the southeast part of the peninsula. Then the water came roaring back in three killer waves from 6.5 feet (2 m) to 23 feet (7 m) in height. In some narrow coves the rocky confines squeezed the waves as high as 88 feet (27 m). The rising ocean floor had somewhat slowed the tsunami, but it still rammed the coast at 60 miles (96.5 km) an hour.

Two hours after an earthquake hit Newfoundland, a tsunami slammed into the Burin Peninsula, sucking seawater away from the coast, then sending the water roaring back in three giant waves. Towns along the coast were pulverized and many homes that were still in one piece were found floating in the sea, as seen in this 1929 newspaper photograph.

Wharves, stages, and flakes were smashed as though made of toothpicks. The waters hurled some fishing boats far inland and carried others far out to sea. Waterfront stores with their valuable contents were snatched away as though by the hands of marauders. Houses were lifted off their foundations. The tsunami deposited some wooden homes on new locations ashore. Others it dragged out to the open sea.

In Lord's Cove, Sarah Rennie had taken little Margaret upstairs after supper to put her to bed. Then she resumed her sewing downstairs. Bernard was still in his high chair, and Rita and young Patrick were quite likely about to do their homework at the kitchen table. Suddenly a wall of water slammed into the house, instantly inundating the lower floor. The house was torn from its foundations and was being sucked out to sea.

At the sound of the thunderous noise, Patrick Rennie and the others who were still at their card game in Prosper Walsh's house ran outside and up a nearby hill. From there Patrick and his sons Albert and Martin could see their home being carried back on the second wave and dumped like so much rubbish in a pond just inside the shoreline. Horrified, the three ran down to the edge of the pond, Patrick shouting Sarah's name and the boys yelling for their mother. From the hill someone urgently called them to come back.

Patrick had apparently become bereft of reason, and was oblivious to everything except that his wife and four children were inside that wrecked house. But Martin realized that another wave might be coming. He took his father by the arm and led him back up the hill. They reached the top before the third wave rolled over the broken remains of Lord's Cove.

Martin had saved his father's life. But what about his mother and siblings? Lord's Cove had been ravaged, and with few exceptions, families had lost almost everything they owned. But the outport people of Newfoundland had a long tradition of sticking together in times of crisis. Putting their own losses out of mind for the moment, a group of men dragged a dory that had survived the carnage over to the pond, and rowed out to the half-submerged house. Through the broken kitchen window they saw that which they had most feared to see. Bernard still sat tied in his high chair, drowned. Rita and little Patrick were dead on the floor. Sarah's body lay near her sewing machine. The men took the sad cargo back to shore, then returned to look for Margaret's body.

The searchers were sure that Margaret would have been in the kitchen with the rest of the family, but they could not find her anywhere on the mud- and seaweed-strewn first floor. Someone said she might be lying on the bottom of the pond. But another man suggested that she could be upstairs.

Gaining access to the second floor was difficult because the house was tilted at a crazy angle and could tip over at any moment. Finally one man was able to climb in through a second-story window. He found Margaret in her bed, covered with mud and kelp. As he lifted the little body he thought he heard a sigh. The child was unconscious, but alive!

The rescuers rowed back to shore as quickly as they could. They took Margaret to a house that had been untouched by the tsunami. There a woman lowered the child into a tub of warm water. Margaret awoke with a scream.

News of the little girl's miraculous survival was greeted with joy throughout Lord's Cove. There was little else for the villagers to be joyful about that night.

Caroline Hillier's father, Thomas, wasn't even supposed to be home that night. He was a fish oil inspector for the government, a job that took him away from Point au Gaul for days at a time, but he had come back early in order to be there for his birthday. Just before the first giant wave roared in from the darkness, he had gone down to the beach to haul his boat onto the shore. The wall of water smashed houses and snuffed out eight lives, including those of three children. Thomas Hillier also died — on the day of his birthday party.

When the first wave swept over Kelly's Cove, it picked up the Brushett house and carried it all the way to the other side of the cove. Inside, Lillian frantically dragged her children out of bed and wrapped them in their coats. Then she and the shrieking children held fast to the bedposts as the second wave seized the house and tossed it back to their own side of the narrows.

After the wild ride had come to a stop, Fred ran to the stairway, only to find it under water. Carrie picked up a chair and hurled it through a window, cutting herself badly on one arm. Then she called out for help.

The desperate mother's cries caught the attention of some people down below, and they hurried to the battered house. By now much of the water had drained out of the lower floor, and Carrie led the children down to the parlor. Lillian still held the warm plate to her throbbing ear. Friends helped them get out through a window and onto the shore.

Carrie and the children hurried to get to higher ground. As they ran for the hill, little Pearl looked back and saw a terrifying sight that she would never forget. Another wall of water was racing in fast, right behind them. With the raging beast in pursuit, Carrie and her children scrambled up the slope. They made it to safety, but as they looked back their house disappeared from sight.

When Marion Kelly heard the deafening roar, she ran out to the yard and saw the mountain of water surging toward her. She snatched up Elroy, went over the fence at the edge of the yard with the agility of a monkey, and sprinted for higher ground. When she looked back she saw her house — with Frances and Dorothy still in it – being dragged out to sea. Neither the second nor the third waves brought it back. Curtis was safe on his hilltop, but the surviving Kelly children never saw their mother and sister again. Not until he returned from the woods a week later would Vincent Kelly learn of the tragedy that had befallen his family.

In Port Au Bras, Tom Fudge and his sons were still working in the family store when Tom detected a powerful smell of seawater and kelp. A moment later he heard the crash of the water as the tsunami tore into the village. Even as Tom rushed to the door, the wave ripped away eleven houses, one of them his own. Tom shouted to his sons to run to high ground. Then, as the waters from the first assault ebbed, he tried to go after the house in which his wife and three daughters were trapped. John took Job to the safety of a hilltop, then he went back down in search of his father. Another villager caught up to the young man and persuaded him to go back up to his brother before another wave came and swallowed him, too.

Later that night, after the power of the tsunami had been spent, John and Job found their father. Incredibly, he was alive. Tom was sitting on the ground near the spot where their house had been, wracked with grief. He had tried to save his wife and daughters, but had been helpless to do anything as the cruel sea took them from him.

From the hill above Lawn, Anna Tarrant and the other villagers watched the first wave smash their community to pieces. As the water washed out, they realized that the home of the two old people who had refused to leave was still standing. Immediately Anna's father, Pat, called on some of his fellow fishermen to follow him. They dashed down the hill and waded through frigid water to the house. This time there was no argument. Pat and his companions carried the old folks up the hill before the second wave struck. Like other communities, Lawn was ruined. But thanks to Pat Tarrant there was no loss of life. Six-year-old Anna, sick with a sore throat and miserable with cold and fear, probably did not comprehend what was happening that terrible night. But she would eventually come to understand that her father was a hero.

In a few short minutes the tsunami had killed twenty-seven people on the Burin Peninsula. Almost half of that number were children. Many of the survivors were left homeless, and had to crowd into the small houses of their friends and relatives. Gone were their supplies of food and winter fuel. Their very means of making a living – wharves, stages, flakes, equipment, and boats – had been pounded to useless wreckage. One Port au Bras fisherman wrote:

"... Everything we have is gone and we are ruined ... everything is dismal and breaks one's heart to look at the harbour and then think of what it was like fifteen minutes before this terrible calamity" (From *Tsunami* by Maura Hanrahan).

Because the telegraph line had been destroyed, it was two days before news of the disaster reached St. John's. Then relief efforts were organized in Newfoundland, Canada, the United States, and Britain. Food, clothing, building materials, and medical aid were soon on their way to the devastated area. But the Burin Peninsula would be a long time recovering.

For the children in Newfoundland outports, the dangers of the sea were a fact of life. Everyone knew that sometimes a father, an uncle, an older brother, or a close friend went out to the fishing grounds and did not come back. But until that night of the tsunami, none would have dreamed that in their own homes they could be threatened by terror from the sea.

10

· · · — — · · ·

THE CHILDREN OF
YANGCHENG
ORPHANS OF WAR

In the spring of 1941, as the horrors of World War II raged, a Japanese army was advancing on Yangcheng, a remote mountain town in northern China. Gladys Aylward, a British missionary, had an almost impossible task ahead of her. She was going to lead a bei (100) of Chinese orphans through the mountains and across the great Yellow River to the city of Sian to keep the children from the approaching Japanese. A government agency had been established in Sian to feed, clothe, and shelter refugee children. Most people would have cringed at the idea of such a journey. But Gladys was no stranger to adversity and peril. She had been severely beaten by Japanese soldiers. She bore the scar of a bullet that had grazed her back. The Japanese had put a price on her head for spying. She was determined that nothing would happen to the children at the hands of the Japanese.

~~~

Gladys found the Japanese soldiers perplexing, to say the least. She had met Japanese officers, and found them to be courteous, civilized, and well-educated men. She had even seen occupation troops mix sugar with water, and serve the sweet treat to laughing Chinese children. But she had also seen what happened when the invading armies of Imperial Japan captured Chinese towns. Burning, looting, and rape! Rampaging troops shot and bayoneted men, women, and children indiscriminately. They tortured anyone they suspected of assisting the Chinese Nationalist Army. Gladys knew a Chinese mule-driver

Gladys Aylward arrived in China as a missionary in 1930 to teach the Christian gospel. The local people called her The Virtuous One.

who had been forced to watch as Japanese soldiers roasted his wife and children alive because he had refused to carry their ammunition boxes.

Gladys had been in Yangcheng in 1938, when Japanese planes appeared in the sky for the first time. People ran out into the streets to look up. Most of them had never seen a plane before. Then the bombs rained down! The destruction inside the ancient, walled town was beyond comprehension. The carnage and chaos were heartrending.

Since then the people had learned to run for cover whenever the planes appeared. Death came not only from the bombs, but also from the fighter planes that screamed down to machinegun anything that moved. One of the boys from Gladys' mission had been shot in the hand and lost three fingers.

Gladys Aylward went to China from England in 1930 to teach the Christian gospel. She based herself in Yangcheng, where she established a mission called the Inn of the Eight Happinesses. This was a waystation where travelers, especially mule drivers who took pack trains through the mountains, could find food and lodging. Gladys would tell her guests stories from the bible. Though she learned to speak the local dialect fluently, Gladys had difficulty at first, because the people there regarded all Europeans as *loo-vang-kwei* — foreign devils!

Her prestige rose when the local governor, called a Mandarin, appointed Gladys as the official Foot Inspector. The Chinese government had outlawed the cruel but ancient practice of binding the feet of baby girls. Tiny feet were considered beautiful, even if the years of binding meant a woman couldn't even walk properly. Now they needed inspectors to make sure the practice was stopped. It was considered shameful for a man to inspect female feet, and Gladys was the only woman in the region whose feet had never been bound. Then Gladys won the admiration of all when she single-handedly quelled a prison riot. After that she was known as *Ai-weh-deh*, The Virtuous One.

Gladys was unmarried and had no children of her own, but her heart went out to the impoverished children of Yangcheng. Girls had it especially hard. Daughters were considered a useless drain on a family's limited resources, and were often abandoned or sold. One day Gladys saw a starving, almost naked urchin in the hands of a woman who was known to be a child-dealer. Gladys bought the little girl with all the money she had on her — the equivalent of

Gladys proved how brave she was by leading 100 children from her orphanage, some of whom are seen here, to safety over rugged mountain ranges and across wide rivers. The march took them a month and the inspiring story of Gladys and the children was made into a movie many years later.

nine English pence. The girl was named Mei-en (Beautiful Grace), but was always called by her nickname, Ninepence.

Soon other children were finding a home at the Inn of the Eight Happinesses. Ninepence came in one day with a little orphaned boy. She told Gladys that if the boy could stay, she would eat less food so that there would be some for him. For want of a better name, Gladys called the boy Less.

Yet another who found a welcome at the inn was Sualan. She was a girl who had been raised as a slave in the household of the Mandarin. With the enemy army approaching, the Mandarin had to move his family to a safer location. Female servants were being dispersed to villages throughout the countryside, but Sualan had no place to go. Gladys happily took the girl into her care.

The disasters that always accompany war swirled through and around Yangcheng as the Japanese and Chinese Nationalist armies battled for control of the town. It was a war fought with modern weapons and primitive savagery. There was no Geneva Convention to protect civilians from atrocities. According to the Japanese philosophy of the time, the Chinese were an inferior race, fit only for servitude. The Chinese government was enforcing a "scorched-earth" policy. Nothing of use was to be left for the invaders. Houses were destroyed. Fields of millet, the staple grain in that part of China, were put to the torch. Caught in the middle of the violence and devastation was an ever-growing horde of parentless, homeless, starving children. Gladys saw it as her duty to save as many of them as she could.

When Gladys assembled her children that first morning of the long trip to Sian, she knew in her heart that the journey would be horribly difficult. And what was even worse was that she had no real idea of how she would accomplish it. She could not even guess at how many miles they would have to travel, because they could not use the known roads and footpaths. The Japanese watched those. Even in the hills, there was the danger of Japanese patrols.

Japanese soldiers were not the only armed men roaming those wild places. Chinese Communists, intent on overthrowing the Chinese Nationalist government, battled with both the Japanese and Chinese Nationalist troops. And, as they had been since time immemorial, the hills were crawling with bandits.

Fewer than twenty of Gladys' girls, including Ninepence and Sualan, were "big;" that is, between the ages of 13 and 15. The feet of some of these girls had been bound in their infancy. Though the bindings had long since been removed, their feet were poorly developed. For them, a long hike across rough country would be a painful trial.

There were only seven "big" boys, aged 11 to 15. The rest of the children were younger, some of them only 4 years old. They laughed, shouted and scampered around as Ai-weh-deh and the older children tried to organize them into columns. They thought they were going on a grand adventure. For the first leg of the journey, the Mandarin had provided two porters carrying baskets of millet. Once that food was gone, Gladys and the children would have to fend for themselves.

Gladys took a final look at the bomb-damaged Inn of the Eight Happinesses that had served for a decade as home, mission, and orphanage. Then she gave a shrill blast on her whistle. The noisy little army of children took their first steps on the road to Sian.

For the first few miles it was all Gladys and the older children could do to keep the little ones together. Small boys ran ahead, or clambered up the rocks along the trail. Gladys had to keep blowing her whistle to bring them back. But as the day wore on and they climbed higher into the hills, the children began to tire. They asked Ai-weh-deh to take them back to Yangcheng. Soon Gladys and the big boys were carrying small children who were too tired to walk. Some of the big girls were limping on their ruined feet.

At sundown they reached a mountain village where an elderly Buddhist priest invited them to spend the night in his temple. The children ate boiled millet, then curled up with their blankets on the floor to sleep. It was not a peaceful night. The temple was infested with rats! For about an hour the big boys tried to keep the squeaking rodents away. Then they, too, gave in to exhaustion and lay down to sleep. The children slept with rats running over and around them.

For the next week they continued across the rugged terrain. Sometimes they found shelter for the night in a village, but often they slept on a mountainside, exposed to cold and rain, and fearful of wolves. In the daytime, Gladys' greatest worry was that they would be spotted by Japanese planes and strafed with machinegun fire.

Sharp rocks soon shredded the cloth shoes they wore, and the big boys had to take turns carrying small children piggyback. Everyone's feet were cut and blistered. The little ones could no longer carry their own bedrolls, so the older children had extra burdens.

They had no guides to show them the way through this sparsely inhabited country. Two boys, Teh and Liang, scouted ahead looking for trails. They marked the way with a bucket of whitewash some villagers had given them. Sometimes the slopes the children had to climb or descend were so steep that they formed a human chain and passed the little ones along hand-over-hand.

When the supply of millet ran out, the two porters turned back for Yangcheng. Now Gladys and the children had no food. Water was a problem, too. The only wells were in villages. In the mornings, as the mountain mists rose, the children would try to wet their tongues with moisture that dripped from the rocks.

They were a week out of Yangcheng and the children were hungry, thirsty, and filthy. Gladys tried to cheer them with hymns, but the little ones cried often. Gladys found that she herself felt unusually weak at times. She was only 5 feet (1.5 m) tall, but had always been a healthy, energetic woman, able to endure hard work and scanty rations.

In the early evening of that seventh day, as the children lay in clusters on a mountainside, Gladys was on the verge of despair. They needed help – and soon. Suddenly Teh and Liang, who had been scouting the trail, came running back. One of them shouted, "Soldiers!"

A cold panic seized Gladys. She put her whistle to her mouth to blow the signal that would tell the children to scatter. But she hesitated. If the children scattered, some of them might become hopelessly lost. Gladys looked down the trail and saw uniformed men come around an outcropping of rock. They were Chinese Nationalist troops!

Barely had the wave of relief passed through Gladys than a new threat struck terror into her heart. The mountainside suddenly echoed with a roar like that of an angry dragon. Overhead were two Japanese fighter planes! Gladys did not have to blow her whistle. The children had been well drilled on what to do in case of an air attack. They dove under rocks, bushes, anything that might hide them. The soldiers also sought cover. The fighter pilots either did not see the people on the mountainside or did not have time to waste on them. The planes thundered past, then disappeared from view.

The fifty soldiers in the column seemed heaven-sent to Gladys. They opened their packs and shared their food with the children, and camped with them that night. Now Gladys was confident that they would make it to their first objective, the Yellow River.

They did, but only after another five hard days. And when the band of ragged, hungry children walked into the port village of Yuan Ku, they found it all but deserted. An elderly man, too old and tired to run away with the others, told Gladys that the entire population had fled to the other side of the river because the Japanese were coming. They had taken all the boats. He said that she should go back into the mountains.

But Ai-weh-deh had not traveled all this way only to turn back. She led the children to the riverbank. It was a mile (1.6 km) wide, very deep, and fast flowing.

The wide-eyed children had never seen anything like the mighty Yellow River. They forgot their hunger for awhile as they bathed themselves, washed their clothes and played in the shallows. But Sualan asked quietly, "Where are the boats, Ai-weh-deh?" Gladys replied that perhaps there would be one in the morning.

Gladys and the children waited on the riverbank for four days. They lived on scraps of food the older boys scavenged from the empty houses of Yuan Ku. There was only enough to feed the little ones. Always there was the fear that the Japanese would come, and they would be trapped.

Then a small patrol of Chinese soldiers found them. The young officer thought that all refugees had already been evacuated across the river. He was astounded to see 100 children led by a foreign woman camped on the river-bank. He was even more astounded when she spoke to him in his own language. The officer signaled across the river, and a boat put out from the opposite shore. By the end of the day, all of the children had been ferried to the village on the other side. There they were taken into people's homes and fed. Gladys was grateful to finally eat something herself, but she was feeling weaker every day.

The following day, Gladys marched the children a few miles to the town of Mien Chih where there was a railroad station. The local Mandarin met her, and arranged for the children to be taken as far along their route as possible by rail. The children were thrilled when they were told that they were going to ride a train. But none of them had ever seen a train before, or even knew what it was.

The next day they were all lined up on the platform, chattering with nervous anticipation. Then came a noise such as they had never heard in their lives. Around the bend thundered a great, iron monster. It belched fire and smoke. The roar of the engine and the screech of steel wheels rent the air. With great screams of terror the children leapt from the platform and ran off in all directions. It took Gladys an hour to find all of their hiding places and round them up, while the engineer waited patiently. Ninepence, Sualan and a few of the older boys said that *they* hadn't been afraid. They'd only run off because they were trying to catch the little ones, they explained.

The train was full of refugees. There were no passenger coaches; just flat cars with roofs. Gladys put all of the children onto one car, and the locomotive puffed out of Mien Chih. Soon the children were squealing with excitement over the new experience. But there were new wails of fear when the train passed into a long, dark tunnel.

For four days Gladys and the children rode across a wide plain. There were stops at camps where the refugees were given food and tea. Gladys slept much of the time as the flatcar rattled along. She could not understand the weariness that had overcome her.

The train ride ended at a village called Tiensan. A vital bridge had been blown up. If the refugees wanted to catch another train farther down the line, they would have to cross a mountain on foot. Gladys felt her heart sink. She and the children had been on the road for three weeks, most of the time afoot. And now, another mountain!

The terrain was even more hostile than that which they had already crossed, and the children were weak, ragged, and barefoot. Everytime they crossed one windswept ridge, another loomed in front of them. The big boys carried the little ones until they were ready to drop from exhaustion. Ninepence, Sualan, and the other big girls were too weak to carry anyone. Gladys had nothing to feed the children but *mentang,* the water in which the millet had been boiled. By the third day a fear came over Gladys that they would never make it; that she had led these innocent orphans of war to their deaths on a barren mountainside.

Gladys sat down and began to weep. When the children saw that Ai-weh-deh was crying they, too, began to wail. Even the teenagers, who had proven to be courageous young men and women, joined in the chorus of hopeless grief.

Then that spirit arose in Gladys that would not let her accept defeat. She wiped the tears from her face, stood up and said, "Now that's enough, all of you! . . . Let's see who can sing the loudest, shall we?" With Ai-weh-deh leading them in a hymn, the children once more struggled along the rocky road to Sian. That evening they reached a village where they were given food and spent the night in the shelter of a cave.

Two hard days later the children of Yangcheng came down the mountain to the town of Tung Kwan, where there was a railway station. Two men told Gladys that there were no refugee trains, but there was a coal train that went to Hwa Chow, which was on the way to Sian. It ran only at night, because Japanese artillery on the other side of the river fired at it in the daytime.

By the time Gladys received this news, the children had all fallen into an exhausted sleep from which they could not be aroused. She managed to shake Ninepence, Sualan, Teh, Liang, and a couple of other big boys awake. Then, with the help of the two men, they carried all of the sleeping children to the train and placed them on the coal cars. Each slumbering child had a "bed" made in the coal to prevent him or her from falling off. Two older children were assigned to each car to watch over the small children. Then the train rolled off into the darkness.

When the children awakened at dawn, they were delighted to discover that they were once again riding a train. They shrieked with laughter when they saw that the coal dust had turned all of them black. That afternoon they arrived at Hwa Chow.

The children spent several days at a refugee hostel before they could board another train for the four-day trip to Sian. When they finally arrived at the station outside that city, Gladys received the biggest disappointment yet. The gates of Sian were closed. The city would accept no more refugees!

Gladys refused to believe this news when she heard it. She took the children to a refugee camp outside the city walls, then strode up to the gate. A watchman on the wall shouted down to her: "Woman! Go away! The city is packed with refugees. No one comes into the city. Woman, go away!"

Gladys leaned against the closed gate and wept. It had taken them a month to reach this place. What was she going to tell the children?

Rescue came in the form of a refugee aid organization called New Life. Representatives of that group arranged for Gladys and the children to be taken by train to the town of Fufeng, where an old temple had been converted into an orphanage and school. There they were given new clothes and shoes. As far as it was possible in China during those turbulent times, the orphans of Yangcheng would be able to resume some sort of normal life.

Soon after reaching Fufeng, Gladys collapsed and became delirious. She was taken by ox-cart to a Scandinavian-American mission. There she remained in the grip of fever for weeks before doctors could bring her back from the brink of death. All during that incredible journey from Yangcheng, Gladys had been suffering from typhoid fever and from internal injuries she'd received when the Japanese soldiers assaulted her.

Gladys recovered from the disease, adopted five of the children herself, and saw Ninepence get married. But the internal injuries would plague her for many years. She needed surgery that the doctors in China were not equipped to perform. In 1949, on the advice of the mission doctors, Gladys Aylward returned to England.

In London a radio producer for the British Broadcasting Corporation read a short newspaper article that told of a woman missionary who had spent twenty years in China. Thinking that the woman might have a story for his program, he went to see her.

Gladys was surprised that a BBC producer should be interested in her. She insisted that nothing very exciting had ever happened to her. After fifteen minutes of conversation with the man, she admitted that she had "once taken some children across the mountains."

A movie made in 1958, The Inn of the Sixth Happiness, *starring Ingrid Bergman, was based on Gladys Aylward's journey with the children of Yangcheng.*

II

·········· — — ··

CHERNOBYL
FOR GENERATIONS TO COME

At 1:23 AM on April 26, 1986, an explosion ripped open a nuclear reactor at Chernobyl in Ukraine. As flames engulfed the plant, more than fifty tons of deadly radioactive dust and other material escaped into the atmosphere. That was ten times the amount of fallout that had resulted from the atomic bombing of Hiroshima, Japan, in World War II. Firefighters were on the scene quickly, but they were neither equipped nor trained to handle this kind of fire. Nobody warned them of the dangerously high levels of radiation that now enveloped the plant and were blowing across the land. They turned their fire hoses on the blaze, but the streams of water instantly turned to radioactive steam, adding to the lethal cloud that was spreading ever further from the blast site. More than 300 firemen and plant employees were exposed to high levels of radiation. But in 1986 Ukraine was still a part of the Soviet Union. The communist Soviet government enforced strict censorship of the media, so the population did not know what was happening at Chernobyl. Not even the people of Pripyat, a city of 45,000 only a mile (1.6 km) from the nuclear plant, were told of the danger. Within a day 129 people were hospitalized. Thirty-one of them soon died. It was the beginning not only of a death toll that continues to rise, but also of a curse that has afflicted the lives of countless children, many of them not even born at the time of the accident.

~~~

Ten-year-old Dimitri and his parents were awakened in the middle of that spring night by a sound like an exploding bomb. The noise was especially sharp, because they had left their windows open to let in the warm breeze. Dimitri's little spaniel, Boris, had scampered under his bed in fright. Looking from the windows of their home at the edge of Pripyat, the family could see a red glow in the direction of the power plant. Dimitri's mother asked his father, who was an engineer at the plant, if there was any danger. His father said no. The reactor, he explained, had many built-in safeguards. The fire posed no serious threat and would soon be under control. Reassured, they went back to their beds, leaving the windows open.

Hours later, after sunrise, Dimitri and his parents could see a pillar of black smoke billowing from the plant. His father still claimed there was nothing to worry about. Had there been a serious problem, he said, they would have been informed.

When Dimitri and the other children of Pripyat headed for school that morning they saw a strange sight. An unusual slimy substance had been sprayed on the streets. The stuff was ankle deep, and the children played in it as though it were rainwater. They did not know that it was a special solution for cleaning up radiation. Nobody had told them. Nobody had told their parents.

At school the children learned of preparations they would be making for the upcoming May Day games. Then something out of the ordinary happened. Doctors came to the school and passed out pills to the children. When Dimitri got his, he dutifully swallowed it without question. He didn't know that it was an iodine pill, an antidote to radiation poisoning. The doctors also told the children that they must stay indoors. They did not say why.

Because it was Saturday, school was dismissed at noon. The teachers reminded the children that they were to go straight to their homes and remain inside. But it was such a beautiful day that few children obeyed. Some went to the edge of town to watch the smoke pouring out of the reactor. Now helicopters were buzzing around, and that was exciting to watch, too.

Other children ran and played in fields. Girls picked wild flowers to put in their hair. When a helicopter landed nearby in an open lot, Dimitri and some of the other boys waited until the rotors stopped whirling and then went up and touched it. No one stopped them.

They did not know that the helicopter was radioactive. So were the flowers the girls picked, the grass they played on, the very air they breathed. There was radiation in their clothing, their hair, and in their bodies.

When Dimitri finally arrived home, his mother scolded him for being tardy. She said there had been an announcement on the radio about a small accident at the nuclear plant, and everybody in Pripyat was to remain indoors. There was no cause for alarm, but as a precaution all windows were to be kept closed. Anybody who had been outside must bathe and dispose of the clothes they'd been wearing. So, instead of taking Boris for his usual after-school walk, Dimitri undressed and gave his clothes to his mother. She said it seemed a waste to dispose of perfectly good clothes, but like most good Soviet citizens she would do as she was told. Then, when she turned the tap to fill the tub, there was another surprise. No water! Pripyat's water had all been diverted to Chernobyl, where firefighters were still waging a hopeless battle against the flames.

As Dimitri got dressed again, his father came home. He had gone out to see what was happening at the plant, but hadn't been allowed in. Police and soldiers had cordoned off the plant. An officer told him this was just a safety measure, but Dimitri's father heard some other men say that the people who had been working the night shift were being confined in the medical clinic. They also said that all the roads leading to Chernobyl and Pripyat were blocked. No one was allowed in or out.

Now his parents seemed concerned, though they assured Dimitri that nothing was wrong. Dimitri's father started phoning around to ask people he knew if they had any information. Nobody knew anything. One man told him that many of the city's officials had not sent their own children to school that day.

Later, with Boris curled up on the floor at his feet, Dimitri watched through a window as a steady stream of helicopters took turns dumping something on the burning reactor. This was a mixture of sand, clay, lead, and boron, a substance that absorbs neutrons and stops nuclear reactions. Still, that night the sky above Chernobyl continued to glow an angry red.

The following day at 2:00 PM an announcement came over the radio and from loudspeakers throughout the city:

> Attention! Attention! Honorable comrades! Following an accident at the Chernobyl nuclear power station, an unfavorable radiation situation is arising in the town of Pripyat. Today, April 27, beginning at 14:00 hours, it will be necessary to start a temporary evacuation of the town's inhabitants to nearby settlements in the Kiev region.

The announcement went on to say that everyone must take enough clothing and money for two or three days. *Nothing else!* All pets were to be left behind. Everyone would be taken out by buses. No cars were to leave the city.

Dimitri didn't like the idea of leaving Boris alone for two or three days, but he had no choice. While his mother packed some clothes, he put down food for the dog and poured bottled water into a pail for him. Then, as instructed, Dimitri and his parents went out to the street to wait for the buses.

The sidewalks were crammed with men, women, and children, all clutching overnight bags and backpacks. Some children were crying about pet dogs, cats, and birds. A few cried for fathers or mothers who were not being evacuated because they were scheduled to work at one of the reactors still in operation. Dimitri was thankful that his father was not staying behind.

Soldiers wearing protective clothing and masks that made them look like alien invaders strode up and down. They answered no questions, but as soon as a house or apartment building was vacated, they put locks on all the doors. Someone said that was to protect the people's property from looters.

Dimitri's family and their neighbors stood there on radioactive pavement, being bombarded by invisible radioactive isotopes for almost three hours. They had no masks or protective clothing. After awhile, Dimitri began to feel dizzy. His throat hurt. He wasn't aware that he and the other children who had been given iodine pills were among the lucky ones. The medication was protecting them from at least some of the effects of radiation poisoning. But not

An abandoned schoolroom in Pripyat is covered with radioactive dust. Children at the school were unaware that the nuclear blast would ruin the rest of their lives. No one was told that everything around them had become radioactive.

everyone had been able to obtain iodine pills. Much of the city's supply had been taken by communist party officials before the general population even knew there was danger. Now, throughout the waiting crowds people were vomiting or fainting from inexplicable fatigue.

At last the buses rolled into Pripyat — more than a thousand of them. Dimitri's mother and father had to help him to board one, because he was so dizzy he couldn't manage the steps. As he settled into his seat and then laid his head against Mother's arm, Dimitri hoped the next few days would pass quickly. He wanted to be back in his own home with Boris.

When the buses left Pripyat for Kiev and other communities, they were radioactive. The people in them were radioactive. The tires of the buses left radioactive trails on the road surfaces as they sped along the highways. The people of Pripyat would never return to their homes. Dimitri would never see Boris again. So great was the concentration of radiation in Pripyat, scientists estimate that more than 500 years must pass before human beings can safely walk that ground.

More than 17,000 children like Dimitri were evacuated from Pripyat that day. For them, and for millions of other children in Ukraine, Belarus, and other places, the nightmare was just beginning.

The Soviet government still had not informed its citizens of the danger. In Kiev the May Day celebrations went on as planned. Residents of the city of three million turned out to watch the parades and the sporting events, hardly suspecting that they were being showered with radiation. Only the families of officials who knew of the danger were quietly evacuated. Doctors who suddenly found themselves treating patients for radiation sickness were instructed to keep quiet. Government agents went into libraries and removed any books that contained information about radiation.

Nor did the Soviet government alert the outside world. Like the evils escaping Pandora's box, the radiation from Chernobyl spread beyond the borders of the Soviet Union to every country in Europe. On Monday, April 28, scientists in Sweden and Finland noted unusually high levels of radiation in the air. They soon realized it was coming from somewhere inside the Soviet Union. The Swedish government frantically sought an explanation from the Soviet government.

At first the Soviets denied that they'd had a nuclear accident. Then they admitted there had been a problem, but they insisted everything was under control. They refused all offers of outside help.

Inside the Soviet Union the only news of the calamity came in short articles buried in the pages of state-controlled newspapers. Most Soviet citizens still knew nothing about Chernobyl. Not until eighteen days after the accident did the Soviet government officially tell the nation what had happened.

Millions of Europeans – from the Soviet Union to the British Isles – had been exposed to an invisible radioactive cloud that would eventually envelop the globe. Depending on weather conditions, some areas were more severely affected than others. Ukraine and Belarus received the worst direct radioactive contamination, but far beyond their borders people suffered long-term exposure to low-level radiation. In addition, people were drinking radioactive water and milk and eating radioactive meat, fruit, and vegetables.

In the years following the accident, the Soviet government admitted to 255 deaths caused by radiation, including eight children who had died from thyroid cancer, which is caused by radiation. Scientists in other countries believe the toll is undoubtedly much higher; probably in the thousands. Little is known of the long-term effects of radiation on the body, but as children like Dimitri reach adulthood, doctors are seeing a startling rise in the cases of respiratory illnesses, various types of cancer, and a condition called "Chernobyl AIDS," in which the immune system breaks down. Those children have also grown up with an above-average rate of severe psychological disorders and are highly susceptible to drug and alcohol addiction and suicide.

Later, many children like this girl would fall victim to leukemia, attributed to the long-term effects of radiation.

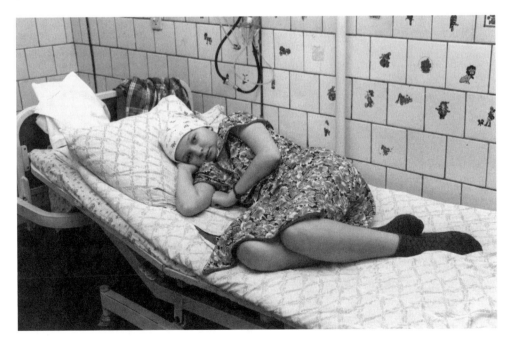

Expectant mothers were horrified when they learned that they and their unborn babies had been exposed to radiation. The Soviet government withheld or falsified so many documents that researchers have had a difficult time determining the effects of Chernobyl on babies who were in the womb when their mothers were exposed. Some believe the exposure was responsible for an increase in the number of children born with leukemia or mental deficiencies, but studies have been inconclusive. However, in Greece, doctors are certain that Chernobyl radiation was responsible for doubling the rate of infant leukemia in their country.

As they reached maturity, many boys of Dimitri's generation were found to be impotent. An extremely high percentage of the girls who eventually became mothers had babies who were stillborn or premature. According to one study, only three percent of the babies born to these women are without abnormalities. Their problems range from jaundice and anemia to frightful physical deformities.

Kofi Annan, Secretary General of the United Nations, indicated the unbelievable magnitude of the Chernobyl disaster in this statement: "At least three million children in Belarus, Ukraine, and the Russian Federation require physical treatment. Not until 2016, at the earliest, will we know the full number of those likely to develop serious medical conditions."

Today vast tracts of land in Ukraine and Belarus are unfit for human habitation or agriculture and will remain so for centuries. The ruins of the Chernobyl reactor have been encased in a concrete shell called the sarcophagus. The contents of the sarcophagus are some of the most radioactively deadly material on the planet, and will remain that way for ten thousand years. Hurricanes, floods, and earthquakes run their course, claim their victims, and then are over. The legacy of Chernobyl will be felt for generations to come.

12

. . . — — . . .

THE TSUNAMI OF 2004
DEATH FROM THE SEA

*A*t about 7:00 on the morning of December 26, 2004, planet Earth shook. *An earthquake with its epicenter at the bottom of the Indian Ocean, just west of the island of Sumatra, registered an astonishing 9.5 on the Richter scale. It was so powerful it caused Earth to wobble in its rotation. The earthquake sent a tsunami racing faster than a jet plane toward the southern shores of Asia and the East Coast of Africa. Scientists in Australia and Hawaii noted readings on their seismic equipment that indicated a quake in the Indian Ocean and sent the information to the nations of South Asia. But because tsunamis are rare in the Indian Ocean, nobody acted on it.*

~~~

That morning 7-year-old Karl was in his family's hotel room at the island resort of Phuket, in Thailand, with his two younger brothers. The boys' parents were outside. Karl and his family were among the 20,000 Swedes enjoying a Christmas holiday in southern Asia, far from the harsh Swedish winter.

At the same time, on an unnamed beach in Indonesia, a crowd of preschool children splashed in shallow, quiet water. In India, 8-year-old Niveda played with her brother and sister in their small coastal Indian village of Singara Thope. On another Indian beach, a group of boys played cricket. Just off Sumatra, a fisherman named Bustami was hard at work in his small boat.

Shortly after 7:30 Bustami felt an unusual movement in the sea beneath him. Less than half an hour later, he watched in amazement as the water rushed back from the shore so suddenly that fish were left flopping around on the bare seabed.

This phenomenon was happening at places all along the coast and around islands such as Sri Lanka. Unaware of the danger, men and boys ran out with pails and sacks to gather up the unexpected bounty. Most of these people lived in poverty, and the opportunity to collect a lot of fish quickly seemed too good to pass up.

But on one beach in India, a fisherman named Chellappa knew something was wrong. "I heard an eerie sound that I have never heard before," he said later. "It was a high-pitched sound followed by a deafening roar. I told everyone to run for their life."

By that time it was too late to run. Along thousands of miles of the coastlines of Indonesia, Malaysia, Thailand, Burma, Sri Lanka, India, The Maldives, and Somalia, giant walls of water were hurtling toward shore at speeds faster than any human could run. Most of the people in the tsunami's path didn't stand a chance.

Bustami heard a noise like bombs exploding. Then his boat was lifted and carried on a wave that was higher than the coconut trees on the shore. He was thrown from his boat, but managed to hold onto the top of a palm tree. He clung to it until he was rescued three hours later.

Everywhere anyone who had run out to gather fish disappeared as mountains of water crashed down on them. The Indonesian pre-schoolers were swept away in an instant. So were the Indian cricket players. Niveda and her brother and sister saw the giant wave coming and ran as fast as they could. They were far enough from the shore that they were able to reach safety, but their home was snatched away by the wave. Tourists who had been snorkeling in the clear blue waters off their resorts were dragged through coral and then dumped ashore, some as far as 2 miles (3 km) inland. Those who had been sunbathing on the beach were carried far out to sea.

As the water surged inland it carried everything before it – cars, houses, livestock, people. Entire fishing villages were completely wiped out. In Kahawa on the south coast of Sri Lanka, fathers ran to put their children on a train called the Queen of the Sea, thinking they would be safe there. Three huge waves smashed into the train, throwing the railway cars against houses and trees like so many toys. Few, if any, of the more than 1,000 people on board survived.

Some adults saw the wave coming in time to grab children and run. But in many cases it was not possible for parents to get *all* of their children to safety. They had to make some horrible split-second decisions. In Banda Aceh on Sumatra, one of the hardest hit places, a mother lost all eleven of her children.

The tsunami was as merciless with elegant resorts as it was with poor fishing villages. Young Karl in Phuket suddenly found his hotel room full of water. He fought to breathe, shut his eyes, and let the waves carry him. When the water receded, the resort had been so thoroughly demolished that Karl thought he'd landed in another town. Some local Thai people found him sitting alone in the wreckage. Karl had a broken collarbone and his feet were badly cut. He was taken to a medical station where his cuts were stitched without benefit of anaesthetic. But that was nothing compared to the pain Karl would feel when he learned that his parents and brothers were gone forever. Karl was eventually returned to Sweden to live with his grandparents.

There were other stories of miraculous survival. A Swedish toddler named Hannes had been with his parents at the Thai resort of Khao Lak. Both parents were swept away, but the little boy was found sitting at the side of a road. Later an uncle saw his picture on the Internet and went to Thailand to take him home. An 8-year-old girl named Juliet spent two days sleeping in the woods before she was found. She had lost her parents and sisters, but also was taken in by relatives. A 20-day-old Malaysian baby was found floating on the ocean on a mattress. She was sunburned but otherwise unhurt. Rescuers took her back to her family. Two Thai brothers, 12-year-old Chaipreak and 8-year-old Chaiya escaped by climbing up trees. They learned later that their mother survived the flood but their father did not.

Twenty minutes after crashing ashore, the waters began to recede. But for the people in the stricken areas trouble was just beginning. Tens of thousands of bodies posed a major health threat. So did countless pools of stagnant water that provided perfect breeding grounds for mosquitoes. Health officials feared outbreaks of diseases such as malaria, cholera, and dengue fever. Almost all facilities for disposing of garbage and human waste had been destroyed, which added to the colossal sanitation problems. Many children were afflicted with diarrhea after drinking foul water.

The dead were everywhere: in the water, on the beaches, in ruined buildings, under cars and trucks, even in trees. Many had been stripped naked by

Two young boys in Banda Aceh, Sumatra, explore the only intact piece of their home after an enormous tsunami devastated the coastlines of many Southeast Asian countries on December 26, 2004.

the sheer force of the waves. Some were horribly mutilated. Others looked as though they had just gone to sleep.

At first, because of the danger of disease, bodies were buried in mass graves or burned on huge pyres before they were even identified. Then the World Health Organization decided that it would help grieving families if they could identify their dead and give them decent burials. Corpses were put in body bags and taken to schools and temples that served as temporary morgues. Experts from the United States and Europe arrived to assist with the identification process. They brought refrigeration units in which bodies could be stored.

Even as the waves were crashing down on the beaches, the outside world was learning of the disaster. Tourists were using their cell phones to call families in Sweden, Canada, and other places to let them know they were alive. Soon the horror could be seen on television news all over the world.

The United States, Canada, Japan, and the other developed nations immediately promised aid. They were quickly told that what they'd promised would be inadequate. Helping the ravaged nations was going to require the biggest relief effort the world had ever seen.

Hundreds of millions of dollars in aid poured into the disaster area. Governments, corporations, private citizens, and even school children around the world contributed. The American aircraft carrier *Abraham Lincoln* and eleven other naval vessels loaded with supplies sailed for Sumatra. Former U.S. presidents George Bush and Bill Clinton personally joined the relief effort and encouraged people to give. Pop stars such as Eric Clapton, Stevie Wonder, and the Barenaked Ladies performed at benefit concerts.

But even with a steady stream of supplies arriving by sea and by air, getting through to desperate people wasn't easy. In many places roads, railways, and telephone lines had been destroyed, leaving communities shut off from the world. Some of them could be reached by helicopter, but others had to wait for help to reach them overland.

A huge challenge facing the various governments and relief agencies was reuniting children with their families. Many of the children who survived the disaster were severely traumatized. Some were so frightened they couldn't speak, making identification difficult. Others couldn't eat or sleep. Photographs of refugee children were posted in public places and displayed on the Internet in hopes that relatives or friends would recognize them.

Many children who had been orphaned were taken in by relatives. There were others, however, who had no one to whom they could turn. Offers of adoption came from around the world. The governments of these children's countries did not feel that it would be right for children who had already suffered harrowing experiences to be suddenly taken away from the culture and surroundings they knew, so foreign adoption was discouraged.

There was another, more sinister group of people interested in the homeless children. Criminals preyed upon these boys and girls by abducting them and selling them into prostitution and slavery. Kidnappers would pretend to be relatives in order to gain custody of children, or would simply carry unfortunate victims away by force.

Parentless children were placed in refugee camps where they could be cared for and watched over while their families were sought or new homes were found for them. The organization called World Vision established Child Friendly Spaces throughout the disaster areas – supervised, safe places where children can play with toys, meet friends, and receive informal schooling. It is an important stepping stone toward physical and emotional recovery after a painful and frightening experience.

The people who live along the coast of South Asia cannot just move away. Unemployment is high in their undeveloped countries. They have to work at the fisheries or in the growing tourist industry. As one man in Sri Lanka said, "Our daily bread comes from the sea. It is our bread and butter. But we are a little bit scared, because we can't control nature."

Because tsunamis were practically unheard of in the Indian Ocean, that body of water had no warning system such as the one operating in the Pacific Ocean where tsunamis are more frequent. A warning system is now being set up in the Indian Ocean in the hopes that the devastation of a disaster such as the tsunami of 2004 will never happen again.

13

· · · · · — — · · ·

HURRICANE KATRINA
DISASTER IN NEW ORLEANS

Like all hurricanes, Katrina was born over the warm waters of the Caribbean Sea. She spiraled north up the route meteorologists call "Hurricane Alley" toward the Gulf Coast of the United States. On August 28, 2005, the National Hurricane Center in Miami classified Katrina as category 5, the highest rating on the scale. This monster storm with winds reaching 175 miles (281 km) per hour was heading straight for New Orleans. Louisiana Governor Kathleen Blanco and New Orleans Mayor Ray Nagin called for an evacuation of the city. Most of New Orleans' 485,000 residents fled, jamming the highway between that city and the state capital of Baton Rouge. But more than 100,000 people remained. Some stubbornly refused to abandon their homes. The majority of those left behind, however, were simply too old, too ill, or too poor to get out of town. For those people the week to come would be a living hell.

~~~

Much of New Orleans is built on a saucer-shaped depression between the Mississippi River and Lake Ponchartrain. This area is actually 6.5 feet (2 m) below sea level. A series of walls called levees protected New Orleans from the river and the lake. On Monday, August 29, 2005, under the relentless pounding of Hurricane Katrina, sections of those levees were breached and 80 percent of New Orleans was flooded. It was this flooding, rather than the hurricane's high winds, that did the most serious damage and caught every level of government almost completely unprepared.

Katrina blew past New Orleans and went on to wreak havoc in Mississippi and Alabama, but she left a disaster area in her wake. Thousands of New Orleans residents were trapped in upper storys of buildings and even on rooftops. They were often without food and clean water, and they were exposed to the heat of the subtropical sun. Because no plans had been made for dealing with a catastrophe of such huge dimensions, help would be a long time coming.

Refugees whose homes had been thoroughly inundated or even washed away poured into already overcrowded centers such as the Louisiana Superdome. There, too, people awaited assistance for intolerable lengths of time amidst increasing squalor. Throughout New Orleans, police and armed forces personnel were diverted from rescue work by uncontrolled looting. Some of the people who broke into stores were only looking for food. But many of the looters took advantage of the disaster to steal anything they could carry off, including guns and ammunition. While these thieves showed the worst side of human nature, other people showed what heroes are made of.

Many of New Orleans' poorest citizens survived because they helped each other while awaiting rescue that seemed as though it would never come. One of the most remarkable stories is that of a 6-year-old boy named De'Mont-e. This child and his mother, father, baby brother, and several aunts, uncles, and cousins were stranded in a second floor, two-bedroom apartment for three days after the hurricane. The electricity was out, and they were running low on food and drinking water. The floodwaters around the apartment building stank. De'Mont-e's mother was extremely worried about the violence that was erupting in nearby streets. She and the other mothers in the building desperately wanted to get their children out of there.

Every day adults took turns going up to the roof to wave bed sheets, hoping to attract the attention of rescue helicopters. But rescue operations were so disorganized that it was Thursday, September 1 before a helicopter finally landed on their building. The National Guardsmen on the aircraft told the stunned parents that they were picking up children only. The adults would have to wait until later. De'Mont-e's mother put his 5-month-old brother, Da'Roneal, in his arms and said, "Don't let him out of your sight." The

6-year-old boy was also put in charge of five younger children, two of them his cousins. Before he climbed into the helicopter, De'Mont-e listened carefully to his mother's instructions.

As the helicopter carried the children across the ravaged city, De'Mont-e looked down and saw entire neighborhoods under water. The other children were crying, but not De'Mont-e. His mother had told him to be "a little man."

For some inexplicable reason the helicopter crew let the children off on a highway overpass that was crowded with people. There was no one in charge, and all were total strangers to the children. De'Mont-e and his group were no better off than they had been on the roof of the apartment building, where at least they had been with family.

De'Mont-e found what seemed to be a safe spot and had all the children sit in a circle, holding hands. He clung to Da'Roneal, and wouldn't let the others go anywhere. He expected the helicopter to return shortly with his parents. It didn't!

Hours later another helicopter picked the children up and flew them to Louis Armstrong International Airport, where they were placed in the care of a medic. De'Mont-e spelled out his full name for the man and gave him his address and phone number. The medic put De'Mont-e and the other children into an ambulance that took them to the city of Baton Rouge.

The children's parents had no idea where they were. There were, in fact, more than 5,000 children who were missing or dislocated in the aftermath of Hurricane Katrina. One young mother was even separated from her newborn child. Thanks to some amazing detective work by the National Center for Missing and Exploited Children (NCMEC) a 2-year-old girl named Gabrielle was reunited with her parents after she identified a photograph of herself as "Gabby."

While the ambulance was taking De'Mont-e and his companions to Baton Rouge, the children's parents were being evacuated in the opposite direction. They were on a bus heading for San Antonio, Texas. As soon as she arrived at the refugee shelter, De'Mont-e's mother began calling the Red Cross, the National Guard, the Federal Emergency Management Agency, and any other organization she could think of, in a frantic search for her sons. On Sunday, September 4, she had a phone call from the NCMEC. Thanks to the information De'Mont-e had provided, that agency had been able to trace the children's parents to San Antonio. The families were soon reunited in Baton Rouge and De'Mont-e was later presented with an award for his courage in keeping the children together in what must have been a very frightening situation.

The chaos and lack of planning was probably at its worst in New Orleans' Louisiana Superdome. The big sports stadium was initially intended to shelter and feed 9,000 people for three days. By the end of the first day of the disaster more than 20,000 people, many of them patients evacuated from hospitals, were crammed into the Dome. And still the people kept coming.

Even before the hurricane struck, a doctor at the Dome had sent out urgent requests for more medical supplies. When Katrina arrived and hurled herself at the big structure, it stood up to the raging winds, but two sections of roof were blown open, allowing rain to pour in. The terrified people inside thought the whole roof was about to go.

Then, as New Orleans was transformed into an extension of Lake Pontchartrain, the electricity went out. Aside from a few flashlight beams and

Rescue helicopters were so overworked and had so many to rescue that often they picked up only the children from groups waiting for rescue. Parents and children were often dropped in different places and even ended up in different cities. It took much detective work to reunite families.

the dim glow of emergency lighting, the Superdome was in darkness. No power meant no air conditioning. The heat and humidity in the stadium became unbearable. People with respiratory problems gasped for breath. Four of them died. Monday passed, then Tuesday, and still people heard no news. Conditions deteriorated as garbage piled up. Rumors circulated that buses would be coming to evacuate them. But no buses came.

By Tuesday night the population in the Dome had swelled to 25,000 men, women, and children. Food and water were scarce. The toilets had become so foul that people were relieving themselves in the aisles. The combined stench of garbage, piles of dirty diapers, and thousands of sweating bodies was overpowering. A television reporter called the Dome "the epicenter of human misery." One doctor complained that he had "sick babies, sick old people, and everything in between."

Most of the storm refugees trapped in that giant sweatbox were well-behaved, law-abiding people. But with the heat, stress, and the overwhelming frustration, tempers were bound to explode. Police officers could not maintain adequate control. There would even be accusations that they didn't make much effort to do so. Some of the young men in the Dome belonged to rival street gangs. Now they claimed their own "turf" in the stadium. Some were allegedly armed with handguns, even though National Guardsmen at the doors checked everyone who entered for weapons.

Governor Blanco visited the Superdome and was appalled at what she saw. She began to make arrangements for the Dome and other refugee centers to be evacuated. First there was a problem in finding buses. Most of the city buses and school buses in New Orleans were under water. The governor had to look for help from transportation companies outside the city. Then there were difficulties in recruiting drivers. The news had been full of stories about looting and violence in New Orleans, so many drivers refused to go there. When at last the buses started to roll into the beleaguered city, before they even got close to the refugee centers they encountered hordes of homeless people sitting at roadsides or taking shelter beneath highway overpasses for the simple reason they had nowhere to go. The authorities reasoned that those people had to be transported

Many children and their parents had to wait days before being rescued from rooftops after the city of New Orleans was hit and flooded by Hurricane Katrina at the end of August in 2005.

to some safe place first. The people in shelters like the Dome would have to wait.

Not until the morning of Thursday, September 1, did the buses begin evacuating the Superdome. Soldiers of the National Guard tried to keep things orderly, but fighting broke out. There were even reports of buses coming under sniper fire. The Guardsmen added to the wretchedness of the situation when they refused to allow people to take pets with them. One little boy attempted to board a bus with a small, fluffy dog named Snowball. He was forced at gunpoint to give the dog up. The child was so upset he cried "Snowball! Snowball!" until he vomited.

The complete evacuation of flooded New Orleans took several days. People stood in 100 degree F (37° C) heat for hours on end waiting to get on buses. Many suffered from hunger and dehydration. One man wanted to know why the United States could send relief to disaster areas all around the world, but couldn't get food and bottled water to a stricken American city. Another man lamented, "We are a Third World city in a First World country."

Other states and countries had in fact been sending food, water, medicine, clothing, and volunteers to New Orleans and other communities that Katrina had savaged. But in the early days of the disaster the flow of aid to Louisiana became bogged down by inefficiency and disorganization. In contrast, refugees who were taken to the Astrodome in Houston, Texas, found the temporary shelter well stocked with food and everything else they would need. It was staffed by relief workers who knew their jobs. Doctors and other health professionals were there to care for the sick, and police officers kept order. The horrors of the Superdome were not repeated. When the Astrodome was filled to its capacity of 15,000, other locations were made available in Houston. Other Texas towns and communities in Arkansas also opened their arms to those made homeless by the storm.

Meanwhile, engineers began to plug up the breaks in the levees and pump out the flooded areas. There was a setback when Hurricane Rita roared into the Gulf Coast on September 23, but eventually New Orleans was pumped dry. It was, however, a ruined city that emerged from the deluge. Hundreds of thousands of homes were either totally destroyed or rendered uninhabitable. Most of the population was billeted in other cities and other states. Some people who had lived in New Orleans all their lives said they would never go back. They had already found jobs in their new communities and registered their children in new schools.

Hurricane Katrina's death toll is placed at about 1,800. Some victims were listed as missing and presumed dead, and were probably swept out to sea. The one bright spot in this great tragedy was that the NCMEC, over a period of several months, found every single missing or dislocated child. As little De'Mont-e's mother put it upon being reunited with her children, "That was the best moment right there. That was all the headache gone, being able to try and pick up your pieces once you're reunited with your kids."

Katrina was one of the most powerful storms to hit the Gulf Coast in recorded history. Nonetheless, many people believed that much of the damage and loss of life in New Orleans could have been prevented. Scientific studies made after the storm showed the design and maintenance of the levees were substandard. All levels of government came under heavy criticism for inadequate planning before the disaster, and failure to respond quickly and efficiently to the needs of victim.

FURTHER READING

Benedict, Michael (Ed.), *In the Face of Disaster* (Viking: Toronto, 2000)

Brinkely, Douglas, *The Great Deluge* (William Morrow Books, New York, 2006)

Brown, Roger David, *Blood on the Coal* (Lancelot Press, Hantsport, NS, 1990)

Burgess, Alan, *The Small Woman* (Evans Brothers, London, 1957)

Cheney, Glenn Alan, *Chernobyl* (New Discovery Books, New York, 1993)

Condon, Judith, *Chernobyl and Other Nuclear Accidents* (Raintree Steck—
    Vaughan Publishers, Austin, TX 1990)

Editors of Time, *Hurricane Katrina: The Storm That Changed America* (Time
    Warner, New York, 2006)

Hanrahan, Maura, *Tsunami: The Newfoundland Tidal Wave* (Flanker Press,
    St. John's NF, 2004)

Higgins, Robert, *The Wreck of the Asia* (University of Waterloo Press, Waterloo
    ON 1995)

Looker, Janet, *Disaster Canada* (Lynx Images, Toronto 2000)

Macdonald, Laura M., *Curse of the Narrows* (Walker & Co., New York, 2005)

McCullough, David, *The Johnstown Flood* (Simon & Schuster, New York 1968)

Metson, Graham, *The Halifax Explosion* (McGraw Hill Ryerson, Toronto,
    1978)

Mannon, Mary Ann, *Miracles & Mysteries: The Halifax Explosion* (Lancelot
    Press, Hanstport, NS, 1977)

Morria, Ann and Larson, Heidi, *Tsunami: Helping Each Other* (Millbrook Press,
    Minneapolis MN, 2005)

Rasky, Frank, *Great Canadian Disasters* (Longman's Green & Co., Toronto 1961)

Stein, Leon, *The Triangle Fire* (Carrol & Graff/Quicksilver Books, New York
    1982)

Stewart. Gail B., *The Tsunami of 2004* (Lucent Books, New York 2005)

Ward Kaari (Ed.), *Great Disasters* (Reader's Digest Books, Pleasantville/
    Montreal 1989)

Zebrowski, Ernest, *The Last Days of St. Pierre* (Rutgers University Press, New Brunswick, NJ/London, 2002)
Periodicals
Child View magazine (World Vision)
The *Toronto Star*
Time magazine

PHOTO CREDITS

Page 9: *Miss Christy Ann Morrison*, S.J. Dixon, Library and Archives Canada, accession numbers 1979–040 NPC, PA-120552.

Page 20: *Sightseers on rooftops, 1889.* Courtesy of the Johnstown Historical Society.

Page 21: House with tree inside, The Camera Shop, Johnstown, CPH 3a47000. Prints and Photographs Division, The Library of Congress, Washington, DC.

Page 26: *A fourteen-year-old coal miner*, Private source, Library and Archives Canada, accession number C-030945.

Page 34: *Boy looking at volcanic damage*, Ph. A Heilprin. F2081 .H45 FOLIO. Prints and Photographs Division, The Library of Congress, Washington, DC.

Page 45: Lillian Clark and family, Glenbow Archives, NA-586-1.

Page 47: Rescue team standing in rubble, Glenbow Archives, NA-586-2.

Page 52: The Triangle Factory Fire, March 1911. Franklin D. Roosevelt Library. New York, NY, March 25, 1911. *Copyright: Brown Brothers.*

Page 53: Skeleton rising from the smoke of the burning Asch building, 1911. 5780 P box 39 ff 18i. Unite Here Archives, Kheel Center, Cornell University.

Page 65: MacDonald, Laura. Photo of Annie Liggins, pg. 191. *Curse of the Narrows*. Walker & Company, New York, NY. 2005.

Page 66: *Save the Blind*, sketch by Arthur Lismer.

Page 73: *L'intérieur du théâtre Laurier-Palace après son incendie*. www.bilan. usherbrooke.ca/bilan/pages/photos/2594.html

Page 80: The Rooms Provincial Archives, A2-149, *Tidal wave disaster, Nfld, Nov. 1929*,/S.H. Parsons & Sons [postcard, number 351], Provincial Archives photograph collection.

Page 86: Burgess, Alan. Gladys Aylward, *The Small Woman*. Evans Brothers, London, 1957.

Page 87: Burgess, Alan. Gladys Aylward and children, *The Small Woman*. Evans Brothers, London, 1957.

Page 100: Abandoned school around Chernobyl NPS. Dec., 1999. Pripyat, Ukraine.(c) Greenpeace/Shigaev, Alexander.

Page 102: Courtesy of Glenn Alan Cheney.

Page 107: *Young children of Banda Aceh, Sumatra*, USN image courtesy of IllinoisPhoto.com.

Page 113: Images of Desperation #7, David J. Phillip, courtesy of AP Wide World Photos.

Page 115: Katrina Devastation #22, David J. Phillip, courtesy of AP Wide World Photos.

ACKNOWLEDGMENTS

The author would like to thank the editors of Tundra Books, the Guelph Public Library, The *Toronto Star,* World Vision Canada, and Maura Hanrahan of St. John's, Newfoundland.